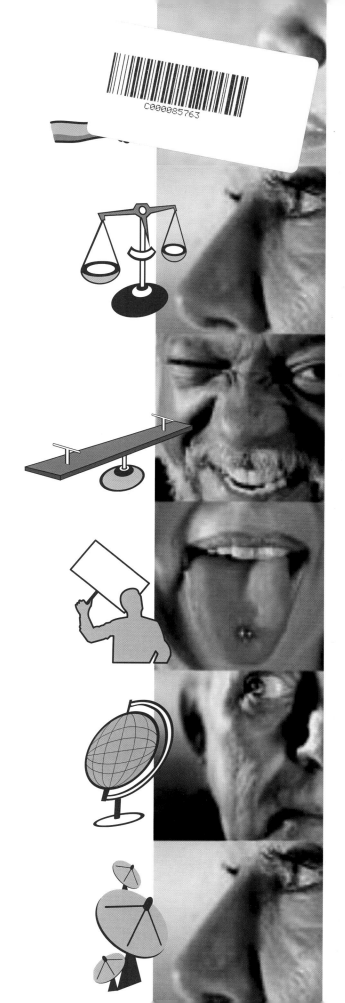

GCSE
Citizenship Studies

Staff Copy 6

Editor: Peter Brett

David Coulson-Lowes
Richard Davison
Elizabeth West
Bernard Williams

© 2002 Folens Limited, on behalf of the authors.

United Kingdom: Folens Publishers, Apex Business Centre, Boscombe Road, Dunstable, LU5 4RL.
Email: folens@folens.com

Ireland: Folens Publishers, Greenhills Road, Tallaght, Dublin 24.
Email: info@folens.ie

Poland: JUKA, ul. Renesansowa 38, Warsaw 01-905.

Folens publications are protected by international copyright laws. All rights are reserved. The copyright of all materials in this publication, except where otherwise stated, remains the property of the publisher and authors. No part of this publication may be reproduced, stored in a retrieval system, or transmitted, in any form or by any means, for whatever purpose, without the written permission of Folens Limited.

Peter Brett, David Coulson-Lowes, Richard Davison, Elizabeth West and Bernard Williams hereby assert their moral rights to be identified as the authors of this work in accordance with the Copyright, Designs and Patents Act 1988.

Editor: Sara Wiegand
Layout artist: James Brown
Design: 2idesign
Illustrations: Stefan Chabluk; Andrew Noble Design Team; Jo Blake and Geoff Jones (Beehive Illustration)
Cover design: 2idesign

Index: compiled by INDEXING SPECIALISTS (UK) LIMITED, 202 Church Road, Hove, East Sussex BN3 2DJ.

First published 2002 by Folens Limited.

Every effort has been made to contact copyright holders of material used in this publication. If any copyright holder has been overlooked, we should be pleased to make any necessary arrangements.

British Library Cataloguing in Publication Data. A catalogue record for this publication is available from the British Library.

ISBN 1-84303-287-2

CONTENTS of GCSE Citizenship Studies

Belonging

Aim

This section looks at 'belonging' and by the end of the three case studies you will:

- understand what makes someone a 'British' citizen
- consider what it means to belong to a multicultural society
- analyse what happens when identities clash.

Source A

"Until the late-Nineteenth Century, at least, the majority of people in the British Isles were never simply … possessed by an overwhelming sense of their own identity as Englishmen, as Scotchmen, as Welshmen, or even as Irishmen. As in the rest of Europe, intense local and regional loyalties were always there to complicate and compromise. In practice, men and women often had double, triple or even quadruple loyalties, mentally locating themselves, according to circumstance, in a village, in a particular landscape, in a region and in one or even two countries."

Professor Linda Colley, historian of Britishness (1992)

'Who are you and where do you come from?' is the most commonly-asked question when meeting people for the first time. It seems a simple question, but the answer can be quite complex. You belong to all sorts of communities, and will probably identify with a number of different places and groups.

Citizenship is partly about exploring how society, politics and your community work. But before you can make sense of this you need to work out how you fit into things. Where are your main commitments? How do you and your family 'belong' as British citizens?

TASK

Working with a partner, imagine that you have to describe to a Martian the main features of where you come from, and what your community is like. Brainstorm some ideas, such as the size of your community, its landscape, housing, main employers and available leisure activities. Then, in no more than 100 words, sum up the characteristics of where you live.

GCSE CHECK

| Topical political, social and cultural issues and events | Legal, political, social, economic and constitutional systems and their influence on your community | Set issues in context, summarise a range of views and express own opinion | Develop skills of critical awareness and evaluation |

Source B

These images are taken from a gallery called 'Images of Britain', part of the British Tourist Authority website. The gallery is intended to encourage visitors to come on a virtual tour of Britain.

Source C

These concentric circles show some of the different ways in which you might feel that you 'belong' in Britain. One of the diagrams relates to your identification with 'place'. The other relates to social, cultural or religious forms of identity. You will probably be able to identify with several of these loyalties. Most people have multiple identities.

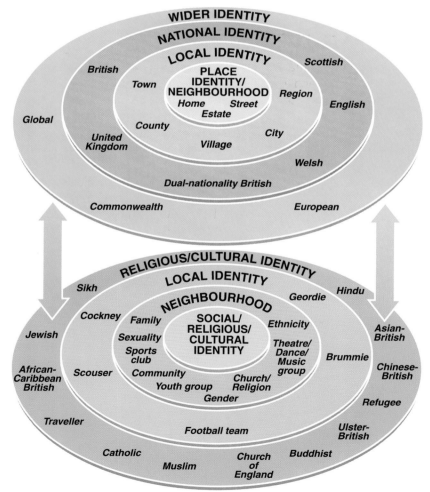

TASK

1. How do you think that the British Tourist Authority decided what images to include on its website? What factors did they have to consider in making their choices?
2. Do the four images provide a fair view of Britain? Think about the strengths and weaknesses of this particular selection.
3. If you had to choose only four images to encourage visitors to come to Britain what might they include? Create a poster, a web page or a PowerPoint presentation using your ICT skills to display your four images. Give a reason for including each one.

TASK

1. Draw your own diagram of concentric loyalties and identities. The diagram has to express the different ways in which you 'belong' to and identify with different kinds of communities and identities. Use the model in Source C for ideas.
2. How is your final diagram similar to and different from those produced by other people in your class? Have you included some loyalties and identities that are not on this model?

Community and identity – what makes you a 'British' citizen?

Aim

You will:

- start to understand the idea of membership and identification with communities
- analyse how Britain represents itself in the most positive light to the rest of the world
- explore some of the major symbols of 'Britishness'
- gain an appreciation of the role of the media in forming opinions on the subject
- consider more local and regional senses of personal identity
- explore positive and negative interpretations of 'Britishness'
- increase your understanding of how different parts of Britain are governed
- develop an improved understanding of what makes you a British citizen.

What makes you a British citizen can be quite hard to pin down. The question of national identity in Britain is more complicated than the geographical and political unit that is called the United Kingdom. Travelling around Britain you soon realise that within national areas there are big variations. For example, Scotland has its own legal and educational systems, and Wales has its own language.

Even inside the biggest nation in the UK, England, there exist significant regional differences. Whatever part of the UK you come from or live in, it is important to know what defines you as a citizen.

↓ **Source A**
The Union Flag can be a cover for less attractive behaviour by English soccer fans.

←**Source B**
Denise Lewis wrapping herself in a Union Flag after winning the gold medal in the Sydney Olympics.

Case Study 1

Symbols of Britishness

This section will explore some of the better-known symbols of 'Britishness', such as the Union Flag, Britannia, John Bull and the British bulldog. National symbols can stimulate powerful emotions. Symbols such as the Eiffel Tower for France, or the Statue of Liberty for America can reveal much about that society's heritage, myths and the common values its people share.

The Union Flag

The Union Flag developed step by step as a symbol of political unity. In 1603 Scotland and England were united when King James VI of Scotland was crowned King James I of England. A new flag was created by laying the English Cross of St George over the top of the Scottish Cross of St Andrew.

The Union Flag emerged after the 1801 Act of Union with Ireland, when the Irish Cross of St Patrick was added to the already complicated criss-cross design. The red dragon of Wales was not represented, possibly as a sign of the historical dominance of England over Wales since the Fifteenth Century.

The Union Flag is also known as the Union Jack, due to its naval connections.

The word 'Jack' was a reference to the 'jackstaff', or flagpole, situated at the stern of Royal Navy ships. The Union Flag remains a powerful symbol of national unity, particularly on occasions such as Remembrance Sunday.

→ Source D
Geri Halliwell and the infamous Union Flag dress she wore to the 1997 Brit Awards as a member of the Spice Girls.

TASKS

1. Explain how the Union Flag is being used in different ways in Sources A, B and D.
2. What are the author's arguments against the Union Flag put forward in Source C?
3. How do you feel about the Union Jack? What for you is the symbol of Britain?
4. What might an updated Union Flag for the Twenty-first Century look like? Would you change the colours, or the design? How would you make it representative of Britain's diverse society?

Source C

"The Union Jack is a conqueror's flag, which owes its design to the subjugation of England's Celtic neighbours and its reputation to the aggressive expeditions which saw Britain steal huge areas of land, labour and natural resources from all over the world. ... Most non-white and Irish people came to Britain wary of the flag already.

When they saw it being displayed by the likes of the National Front they saw it as the logical continuation of the purpose for which it was flown in their mother countries. It was one of the most potent symbols of the arrogance of British colonialism. ... True it is the only flag that Britain has but that is the weakest argument of all. There are several examples, from very recent history, of nations changing their flags."

Adapted from an article by Gary Younge in *Red Pepper*, a left-wing radical magazine (1997)

John Bull

John Bull was a symbol created by authors and journalists in the early-Eighteenth Century. He personified many traits that Englishmen thought lay deep in their common character. He symbolised qualities such as honesty, a love of life and a generous heart. All these were believed to be the features that the people of Britain wanted in a national icon.

Britannia

Britannia was the original name given by the Romans to the province that made up what is now England and Wales. From the Sixteenth Century she became the first personified national symbol – a woman wearing a helmet and carrying a shield and trident. She was seen as representing the values of honour, bravery and justice. She came to symbolise Britain's command over the seas, and is still remembered in the song *Rule Britannia*. She also appears on the 50p coin!

> **Source E**
> "We have the most rotten sort of patriotism in this country which is the result of our imperial past. People in Britain only ever feel able to be positive or feel good about being British if we are beating somebody, whether at war or sport; we have to have the best bands or the best pop music. That's something that people have to get out of their psyche – the idea of conquest."
>
> *Jeremy Hardy, comedian, broadcaster and former columnist for The Guardian, a liberal newspaper*

The bulldog

The bulldog is a British breed of dog created to bait bulls – a sport banned in 1835 – in which the dog grabbed the bull by the nose and hung on at all costs. In 1997 the British Labour Party used a bulldog, a traditional symbol of Britain's strength and tenacity, in a party election broadcast. The dog was required to look tired and fed-up, but cheered up when Tony Blair explained his 'vision for the future'. Historically, the bulldog mascot has been more frequently associated with the Conservative Party, Winston Churchill and the Second World War. Blair's opponents rejected Labour's claim to be the more patriotic party.

TASKS

1. Why do you think that the images of Britannia, John Bull and the British bulldog have proved so long lasting as symbols of Britishness?
2. In countries like America patriotism is much more directly celebrated than in Britain. Americans commonly display the Stars and Stripes flag on their homes, and hold regular ceremonies to salute the flag in schools.
   a) Why does Jeremy Hardy argue that 'we have the most rotten sort of patriotism in this country'?
   b) Do you agree with him? Give at least three reasons for your answer.

Governing Britain: recent changes

The 129 Members of the Scottish Parliament elected on the 6th May 1999

There have been recent changes in the way parts of Britain are governed, and this is the process of devolution. This has meant the transfer of some powers from the Parliament in London to permanent national assemblies in Scotland and Wales. In Northern Ireland, as part of the peace process, a new assembly has also been elected but, as Case Study 3 shows, this has not been without difficulties. The Assembly has at times been suspended and 'direct rule' from Westminster used in its place.

One aim of devolution is that decisions are taken at a more local level. This might be at the Scottish (country) level, or it might be a big city. For example, the people of London have been given more powers to decide things for themselves through the creation of a Mayor for London.

However, it is still Parliament in London that decides how much power these assemblies can have. Questions of foreign affairs, defence, taxation and most economic matters, levels of social security benefit and broadcasting are still decided for the whole of the UK by the government in London.

Examples of devolved issues include health, education, the environment, housing, transport and some aspects of economic development and agriculture.

Since May 1999 there has been a Welsh Assembly. This has fewer powers than the Scottish Parliament. All laws for Wales are still passed by Parliament in London, although the Assembly can debate and give its views on issues directly affecting Wales. It also has responsibility for deciding how laws on health, education, agriculture, transport, industry, training and the environment are put into practice in Wales.

Factfile

Some features of being British

Anyone born in the UK before 1 January 1983 is automatically a British citizen. After this date you are only a British citizen if either of your parents are British citizens or are entitled to live here permanently. For unmarried parents only the mother's position counts. British citizenship is also possible through naturalisation or registration.

Britain is a multi-national state: a political unit ruled by a single authority, but made up of what used to be historically different nations whose populations maintain distinctive national identities.

The role of the monarch is a distinctive aspect of being British. The crown is the symbol of authority in Britain: the law courts are Her Majesty's Courts, and the government is Her Majesty's Government. The Queen exercises few powers personally but is the formal head of state.

Britain has no written constitution. Instead what we can and cannot do as citizens is defined by statute law (Acts of Parliament), common law (court decisions) and various conventions.

Being British also means being European since the UK joined the European Community in 1973.

Being British also means that you live in one of the few rich countries in an otherwise poor world. This is reflected in life expectancy: in Britain it is 76, but in Africa it is 53.

Britain is industrial: only 2% of the employed population work on the land.

There are striking regional differences in Britain. One argument is about the 'North-South divide', a division between prosperous and poorer parts of Britain. Real incomes in South East England are genuinely higher than in any other part of Britain.

Exploring the nature of Britishness

→ **Source F**
Summary of a speech by Robin Cook, British Foreign Secretary, on 'Britishness' (April 2001).

TASKS

Look at the summary of the speech by the British Foreign Secretary.

1. Political opponents might argue against all three of his main points. Working in groups, come up with as many arguments as you can which disagree with the Foreign Secretary's arguments.

2. Why do you think that Robin Cook made this speech? Think about his job, party political considerations, his arguments, the timing of the speech and his sincere convictions.

3. Robin Cook provides an optimistic framework here of what it means to be British. You may not agree with everything he says, but can you provide a better definition of 'Britishness' in about 300 words?

Reasons for being optimistic about the future of Britain and Britishness

1. He denied that British identity was under siege from the arrival of immigrants who do not share 'our' cultural values. The reasons he gave were:

a) Britain has always been "a gathering of countless different races and communities, the vast majority of which were not indigenous to these islands" – for example, Romans, Normans, Vikings, Jews and communities from the Caribbean, Asia and Africa.

b) Pluralism (a mix of many peoples and cultures) is "an immense asset" and not a problem. Linguistic diversity is good for attracting foreign companies to invest in Britain. Immigration is necessary to meet economic demand for skilled workers.

c) New communities have broadened our cultural horizons. "Chicken tikka masala is now a true British national dish, not only because it is the most popular, but because it is a perfect illustration of the way Britain absorbs and adapts external influences. Chicken tikka is an Indian dish. The masala sauce was added to satisfy the desire of British people to have their meat served in gravy."

d) "The modern notion of national identity cannot be based on race and ethnicity but must be based on shared ideals and aspirations." For example, some of the most successful countries in the world, like America and Canada, are immigrant societies. They show how the idea of equal citizenship can be a source of strength.

Source G
"Should we be proud or appalled, that the chicken tikka masala has become the cultural symbol of our times? The dish has no genuine provenance. When abusive customers burping lager, stagger in, the restaurant owner and his staff know what's in store. More lager *Gunga Din*! More popadoms! Onion bhajis and chicken tikka masala. Someone will order a vindaloo for a laugh. The waiters have their accents mimicked. They are physically threatened if they refuse to serve more alcohol to a group who are singing and cheering as if in a football stadium. In this light our emblem of multiculturalism starts to look a bit murky. Eating curry and breaking down racial barriers are two entirely different things."

Extract from an article by Iqbal Wahhab in The Independent, *(24 April 2001)*

Is chicken tikka masala a good metaphor for Britain being a successful multicultural society?

2. He denied that British identity was under threat from membership of the European Union on the grounds that:

a) Britain is European in terms of both its geography and history – "our 'culture', our security and our prosperity are inseparable from the continent of Europe".

b) There is no real alternative association other than the EU.

c) It is important to work together with other European countries on international issues such as the environment, the fight against organised crime, policy on asylum and European stability.

d) Britain shares European assumptions about how society should be organised, for example approaches to social justice.

e) No European partner, such as France or Italy, feels it is losing its national identity through closer European integration.

f) Belonging to a successful EU will boost rather than undermine national identity. For example, Spain and Greece joined the EU as an expression of freedom from fascism and a guarantee of a democratic future. Ireland has developed a new economy and a new assertiveness of Irish identity and confidence in its culture; "We can see that for ourselves in Britain through the new affection for Irish music and dance and the attachment to Irish pubs."

3. He denied that the devolution of power to Scotland, Wales and Northern Ireland represented steps towards the break-up of Britain because:

a) The votes for devolution were not votes for separation – "they were votes to remain in the United Kingdom with a new constitutional settlement".

b) "Our future together in a single state is all the more secure if we each respect the distinctive identity that makes some of us Scottish and others Welsh or English. That mutual respect strengthens our common identity as British." For example, in Scotland the legal and educational systems are an important expression of 'Scottishness', but at a British level there is a strong attachment to institutions such as the NHS or the BBC.

c) The concept of identity is not mutually exclusive – "it embraces numerous dimensions, each of which serves to amplify and reinforce the others". Taking sport as an example, people watch Scotland, England, Wales or Northern Ireland in football, cheer for the British team at the Olympics and support Europe playing golf in the Ryder Cup.

Source H

"The problem of Britishness is basically a problem of Englishness. There is a tendency to get England and Britain and nation and state all muddled up. The Scots and the Welsh by and large, do not find Britain puzzling. Some of them do not want to stay with it, but at least they know what it is. They are Scottish or Welsh in national identity, British in citizenship."

Extract from an article by Neal Ascherson first published by The Independent on Sunday *(2 April 1995)*

Do you agree that the English have a problem with their sense of identity?

What is it like to live in multicultural Britain?

Aim

You will:

- understand what it means to live in the United Kingdom – a culturally diverse democratic society which ideally values everybody and gives them equal rights
- appreciate the need for mutual respect and understanding between different individuals, groups and communities
- analyse what multiculturalism means for schools and the education system
- understand some of the factors contributing to racial inequalities
- support the process of working towards racial equality.

Modern Britain is a multicultural, multi-ethnic, multilingual, multiracial society.

This ethnic diversity is a strength. Since the Second World War immigrants have brought fresh ideas, new skills, labour, money to invest and a range of cultures that make the country richer and the lives of its people more varied. People in Britain have many differences, but they inhabit the same space and share the same future. All have a role in helping to make Britain an outward-looking and generous society that values all its citizens.

←Source A
London's Notting Hill Carnival: a British festival where everyone is welcome.

The Commission on the Future of Multi-Ethnic Britain in 2000, made up of leading members of minority ethnic groups, concluded that "Britain is a community of communities, a community with a collective sense of identity most certainly, but also including within it many communities with a more or less developed sense of their own identity".

Their report was controversial. For example, it suggested that the word 'British' failed to define the people of this country in a way that fully included the 3.3 million minority ethnic Britons who make up more than 7% of the population. The Commission's report concluded that the term offered a narrow, often South East England centred, vision of the population. This image failed to recognise the voices, experiences and stories of British people for whom being African, African-Caribbean, Black, Chinese, Indian, Irish, Jewish, Muslim, Punjabi, Sikh, South Asian or Traveller is a central part of their identity.

TASKS

1. Would it be better to speak of modern Britain in terms of a 'community of communities' ?
2. Why do you think that members of minority ethnic groups sometimes feel a lesser sense of 'belonging' within British society?

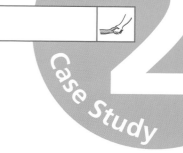
Factfile

The contributions of ethnic minorities

People from minority ethnic groups, and the cultures they have brought with them, are essential to life in Britain today.

- Over two-thirds of independently-owned local shops belong to people from ethnic minorities.

- Black British people contribute £5 billion spending to the economy.

- Since it was established in 1948, Britain's National Health Service has depended heavily on ethnic minority doctors, nurses and auxiliary staff – about 23% of Britain's doctors were born overseas.

- 24% of restaurant employees were born outside Britain.

- 27% of London Underground staff are from ethnic minorities.

- Some of Britain's best sports stars are of African-Caribbean or Asian descent.

- British literature, art, music, dance and theatre are enriched by people who can draw on a wide variety of cultural influences.

TASK

List as many positive aspects of living in multicultural Britain as you can which relate to your own experience.

Source B

"Separate educational arrangements, community and voluntary bodies, employment, places of worship, language, social and cultural networks, means that many communities operate on the basis of a series of parallel lives. ... We believe that there is an urgent need to promote community cohesion, based upon a greater knowledge of, contact between, and respect for, the various cultures that now make Great Britain such a rich and diverse nation."

From a Home Office Report on 'Community Cohesion' (December 2001)

Key words

citizenship — the state of being or of having rights and responsibilities as a citizen; and conduct in relation to these duties

community — an organised political or social body; a body of people in the same locality and group, having work and interests in common

diversity — the quality of being diverse; a difference, distinction, variety

ethnic minority — an immigrant or racial group regarded by those claiming to speak for the cultural majority as distinct and unassimilated

integration — the bringing of parts together into a whole; the removal of barriers imposing segregation upon, for example, racial groups

TASKS

1. Working in groups, take each of the key words and rewrite the explanation in words that you understand more easily. Share your thoughts with other groups.

2. Read Source B. Differences between cultural groups can lead to problems but can also be something positive and enriching. In your groups make four suggestions of actions that might help different cultural groups to integrate into a wider community.

Schools and racial equality

At their best, schools can present a picture of a multicultural society that works: harmonious, happy and purposeful, where the riches of every culture and every individual are valued. Schools can play a vital part in contributing to the development of a socially just, inclusive society. For example, some schools in largely white areas have adopted multicultural or anti-racist policies with the explicit aim of challenging racist stereotyping and behaviour among white pupils. The role of schools is to help pupils to become informed, concerned citizens and to increase mutual understanding, respect and appreciation of cultural diversity. The introduction of Citizenship to the National Curriculum in September 2002 provided a unique opportunity to promote education for racial equality.

In England as a whole, minority ethnic groups make up 11.3% of the population of schools that are funded through the local education authorities (although there are big variations between different areas of England). A country's education system is a gateway to employment and to participation in political, social and cultural affairs. Also, it equips young people – or fails to equip them – with the essential understanding, skills and values which they need in order to play a substantial role in the building and maintenance of Britain as a community of citizens and a community of communities.

Source C

"A five-year-old Sikh boy had eagerly anticipated starting primary school. Within months of his being a pupil at the school, he had radically changed from being active, bright and outgoing, into a withdrawn child no longer communicating with anyone, wetting himself and having nightmares. A few sessions at the clinic revealed that he was frightened to go to school because other children jeered at him, often pulled his hair and ridiculed his grandparents who brought him to school every morning. The school did not seem to consider that it was its responsibility to challenge the racist behaviour of the pupils and so did nothing. The headteacher advised parents to transfer him to another school where there were more 'Asian' children."

All our Children by Babette Brown
BBC Education (1995)

The Chairman of the Commission for Racial Equality has argued that the British education system is 'institutionally racist'. Many pupils and teachers will find this view surprising. Schools are committed to values such as human rights, justice, equality and fairness, all of which lie at the heart of Citizenship. So what is the evidence for racism?

Source D

"Teaching young people the value of diversity and a proper sense of society and their place in it potentially offers great benefits in tackling racism and promoting race equality. This is something I resolutely believed during my term as Secretary of State for Education and Employment and it is why I introduced Citizenship Education to the National Curriculum. Our aim is to help achieve a wider vision – a vision of a successful multicultural Britain, where every citizen and every community earns and gives respect."

From an article in *Connections* (a magazine produced by the Commission for Racial Equality) by David Blunkett, Home Secretary (summer 2001)

TASKS

1. Do you think that Citizenship education can have the positive effects outlined by David Blunkett? Give at least three reasons for your answer.
2. What would have been a better way of dealing with the bullying faced by the five-year-old Sikh boy?

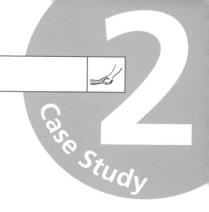

Schools and institutional racism

A list of the possible features of institutional racism within the education system might include some of the following.

- Over-representation of black and other minority students among those excluded from school, particularly African-Caribbean boys and girls, who are six times as likely to be excluded from school as their white counterparts.

Experts find it hard to work out the various reasons for this but it is a worrying statistic.

- Large differences in educational outcomes between ethnic groups in many schools and Local Education Authorities, even when social and economic background factors are taken into account. These affect, in particular, pupils and students from African-Caribbean, Bangladeshi and Pakistani communities.

How can all pupils be encouraged to achieve their full potential?

- Members of Asian and black communities are not recruited as teachers to the extent that could reasonably be expected and, having been recruited, receive less than their fair share of promotion, training and career development opportunities.

Why do you think that there are not more minority ethnic teachers and school leaders?

- Few teachers have skills in inter-cultural understanding and communication and in defusing situations of actual or potential conflict and tension.

Issues here might include faith festivals, religious requirements, dress codes and holidays.

- Schools could do more to seek out the views and perceptions of minority ethnic groups.

What are the opportunities for collaboration?

- Many ethnic minority pupils regularly face direct racism. Racial taunting is a daily experience for many ethnic minority pupils.

Guidance for key stage 4 PSHE states that pupils should be taught "to challenge offending behaviour, prejudice, bullying, racism and discrimination assertively and take the initiative in giving and receiving support". How can this be done?

- Superficial multiculturalism. Schools were criticised in the 1980s for token gestures towards saris, samosas and steel bands. Stereotyping pupils can result in low expectations and under-achievement.

What is an appropriate curriculum?

Adapted from Teacher Training Agency Guidance (2001)

A definition of institutional racism is:

"The collective failure of an organisation to provide an appropriate and professional service to people because of their colour, culture, or ethnic origin. It can be seen or detected in processes, attitudes and behaviour which amount to discrimination through unwitting prejudice, ignorance, thoughtlessness and racist stereotyping which disadvantage minority ethnic pupils."

From *The Macpherson Report* (1999). This report was produced following the murder of the black teenager Stephen Lawrence in London in 1993, and later failures in the police investigation of the case.

TASK

There have been many changes introduced in recent years to try to improve the situation in schools. There are many teachers, community groups and schools engaged doing good work in relation to race equality and cultural diversity. If you were a government adviser, what advice would you give to help create a fairer deal for ethnic minority children within Britain's education system? Use the questions and comments on the left to help to structure your thoughts.

Origins of ethnic diversity

Many different ethnic groups live in the UK. Some of these mixed together long ago, when peoples such as the Angles, Saxons, Vikings and Normans invaded the islands from mainland Europe. Celtic peoples include the Welsh, Scots, Irish and Cornish. The largest ethnic group in Britain is formed by the English, who are closely related to Germanic peoples such as the Dutch and Germans.

Others to have settled in the UK include Roma (often known as gypsies), Jews and peoples from Central and Eastern Europe. More recently, many British people are descended from families who originally came from more distant parts of the world that were once part of the British Empire. For example, Indians, Pakistanis, Bangladeshis, Hong Kong Chinese, African-Caribbeans and Ugandans.

Racial inequality

It is against the law for an employer to discriminate against someone because of their race, colour, country of origin or ethnic group, as explained in the Race Relations Act 1976. A further Race Relations Act 2000 made racial harassment and racially-motivated violence specific criminal offences. Nevertheless, large numbers still experience discrimination in their dealings with the police, employers, schools and health services. Many also face lives blighted by poverty.

Organised racist groups are weaker in Britain than in the rest of Europe, but the fact that open and institutionalised racism persists in liberal societies – including Britain – means that the whole foundations of democracy and citizenship can be constantly undermined.

- 60% of people of Bangladeshi or Pakistani origin in Britain live in poverty.
- More than half of Britons of African-Caribbean and African background live in districts with the highest rates of unemployment.
- Racism and discrimination are not confined to 'visible' and established minorities, but other individuals and communities including asylum seekers, Jewish and Irish people and travellers.
- Research from the Commission for Racial Equality, taken from a number of anti-racist studies from across the Midlands, shows that up to 50% of perpetrators of racial harassment are under the age of 17.

↑ **Source E**
A local newspaper captioned this photograph 'The Scene on Bradford's Front Line', following race riots in the summer of 2001.

Taking a stand against racism

There are a variety of ways in which you might take an active stand against prejudice, discrimination and racism. You can find out more about anti-racist campaign groups such as the Anti-Nazi League (ANL), Show Racism the Red Card, Me Too, National Assembly Against Racism, Campaign Against Racism and Fascism or Searchlight. The ANL suggests the following as possible campaigning tactics:

- leafleting and petitioning in local shopping centres and housing estates
- demonstrations and protests
- organising to prevent a platform for the spread of racist ideas
- teaching anti-racism
- graffiti: Nazi and racist graffiti can appear in many places. Can you organise a group to paint out and clean it up?
- music: from Rock Against Racism in the 1970s to the ANL Carnival in 1994, music plays an important role. Numerous local raves against racism are held.

TASKS

1. Look at Source F. What problems for race relations in Bradford are identified?
2. List the reasons why people may hold racist thoughts or beliefs.
3. In what ways are racism and racial inequality an issue in your local area?
4. Draw at least three conclusions from Source G.
5. Working in a group, decide which of the tactics against racism suggested by the Anti-Nazi League you think are the most effective. Rank your decisions from 1–6 and justify the order to the rest of the class.

"Race relations in Bradford are deteriorating, with communities becoming increasingly isolated along racial lines and segregated schools fuelling divisions, according to an official report. ... The 11-strong panel, chaired by Sir Herman Ouseley, the former head of the Commission for Racial Equality, interviewed all sections of the city's population between November 2000 and April 2001. ... Its most worrying conclusion ... is that Bradford's race relations are going into reverse.

The key concern is that relations between different cultural communities should be improving, but instead they are deteriorating. There are signs that communities are fragmenting along racial, cultural and faith lines. The report estimates that the population of Pakistani Muslim heritage is 15% of the city compared with 10% in 1991, making them the largest group out of Bradford's 22% ethnic minority population. ... Victims of discrimination get inadequate support, people believe, and 'Islamaphobia' is regarded as prevalent in schools. The inquiry also found concern about discrimination in the labour market against Asians. Disillusionment is found to be especially high among young people."

← **Source F**
From *The Guardian*
(10 July 2001)

↓ **Source G**
Unemployment rates in the working population.

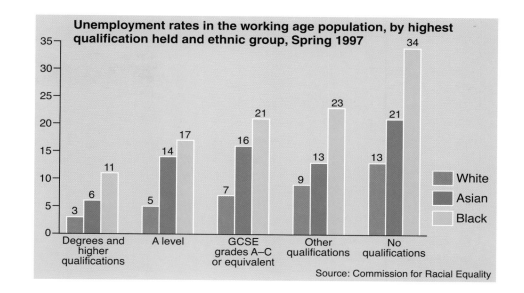

Unemployment rates in the working age population, by highest qualification held and ethnic group, Spring 1997

Qualification	White	Asian	Black
Degrees and higher qualifications	3	6	11
A level	5	14	17
GCSE grades A–C or equivalent	7	16	21
Other qualifications	9	13	23
No qualifications	13	21	34

Source: Commission for Racial Equality

Class commission on multicultural Britain

TASK

You have been appointed by government ministers to a small working group of advisers (four or five people) to make recommendations in the seven areas of policy outlined below. Your task is to make detailed suggestions as to how policies, laws, attitudes or values can (or should not) be changed in the seven areas in the table below. The overall aim is to create a fairer and more representative multicultural society. You can then make one more additional recommendation for change unrelated to these seven areas.

Area of discussion	Background
Equality	Equality of opportunity has been the law in Britain since the mid-1970s but Britain is still a long way from being an equal society.
Politics and representation	There are a very small number of minority ethnic MPs in Parliament.
Employment	Minority ethnic groups get an unfair deal when it comes to employment, whatever their qualifications (see Source G).
The armed forces	In 1994 Mark Campbell left the Life Guards after his bed was soaked in urine and he was left a note saying, 'There is no black in the Union Jack'. The army is now doing its best to both improve its image and address the racism within its ranks. But it remains an unattractive prospect for Britain's ethnic minorities. Only around 1% of the British armed forces come from ethnic minorities.
The police force	The police were described as institutionally racist in a recent official report following an inquiry into their methods during the Stephen Lawrence case.
Faith schools	There is pressure to establish more of these, for example from within the Muslim and Sikh communities. There are many Church of England and Catholic schools. But will more faith schools promote greater tolerance and mutual understanding?
Tackling economic disadvantage	Minority ethnic communities are often (but by no means always) at the bottom of the economic pile. What can be done to counter economic injustice for minority groups?

←Source H
To what extent should faith schools be encouraged within a multicultural society?

→Source I
How can the police force and the armed forces generate more support from minority ethnic groups? How can they change to become more representative of Britain's multicultural society?

TASKS

1. Your working group now has to present and then defend its conclusions from the previous task in a press conference. After each group has presented their recommendations, everyone in the class (or press room because you are all 'in role' as journalists) should write down two questions that they would like to ask the group.

2. It is important to reflect on the process of what you are learning in whole-class discussions and debates:
   a) What did you like and dislike about the debate?
   b) What did you learn?
   c) Draw up a set of guidelines that you think will enable your class to have better discussions in the future.

GCSE CHECK

Comment upon topical and controversial issues	Knowledge and understanding of 'belonging' in multicultural Britain	Implications of cultural diversity for you and your community	Weigh up opinions and make judgements supported by evidence	Critically evaluate a citizenship activity in which you have participated	Engage with key concepts such as 'fairness', 'rights', 'justice', 'equality' and 'freedom'

What happens when communities conflict?
A study of
Northern Ireland

Aim

You will:

- identify some of the key events in the history of the Troubles
- describe and explain the different factors that have made conflict hard to end
- describe the strategies that aim to improve relationships between the different communities.

The Omagh bombing in 1998 came at a time of hope for a peaceful solution to 30 years of conflict in Northern Ireland. It illustrated some of the obstacles to the peace process as well as the costs of failure. In the previous case studies you have examined different factors that can shape the identity of an individual or a community. In this case study you will start to explore how these 'identity shapers' can become a source of conflict. This case study is an introduction to these issues.

Source A

"This appalling act was carried out by those opposed to the peace process. It is designed to wreck the process and everyone should work to ensure the peace process continues."

Martin McGuiness, chief negotiator for Sinn Fein (16 August 1998)

Source B

"This is a dreadful crime against humanity."

Ken Maginnis, Ulster Unionist security spokesman (16 August 1998)

The two traditions

The north of Ireland has experienced 400 years of religious and political conflict. The past 30 years of the Troubles have reflected and reinforced divisions between the majority community, the Protestants, and their Catholic neighbours. However, religious identity has often been linked with a political and cultural identity, and sometimes with an economic identity. These identities are reflected in the murals (see Sources D and E), which in turn clearly mark out whose 'territory' it is.

Source C

National identity in Northern Ireland

Would you describe yourself as:

	1989		1993	
	Catholic	Protestant	Catholic	Protestant
Irish	60%	3%	61%	2%
Ulster	2%	10%	1%	15%
Northern Irish	25%	16%	24%	11%
British	8%	68%	12%	69%

Source: Social Attitudes in Northern Ireland (1995)

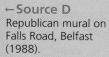
Who's who

Unionists are mainly from the Protestant community. They support the political union of Northern Ireland with Britain. They fear that a united Ireland would ignore their religious and cultural traditions.

The main Unionist party is the Ulster Unionist party, which agreed to the Good Friday Agreement. Other Unionist parties – such as the Democratic Unionist Party – have consistently opposed sharing power with Nationalists and opposed the Good Friday Agreement (see the Timeline).

Loyalists also believe in the continued union with Britain but have used violence to achieve this. Loyalist paramilitary groups – such as the Ulster Defence Association – claim to be defending Protestant traditions.

Nationalists are mainly Catholic. They hope for a united Ireland, independent of Britain. Many feel as second-class citizens within Northern Ireland. The main Nationalist party in Northern Ireland is the Social Democratic and Labour Party (SDLP). It is opposed to the use of violence, and has used legal methods to achieve its aims.

Republicans also want a united Ireland. They have viewed British troops in Northern Ireland as a force of occupation. Sinn Fein is the legal political party associated with Republicanism. It signed up to the Good Friday Agreement. The Irish Republican Army (IRA) has been the main Republican paramilitary group attacking British targets and Loyalists. Sections have split off in anger at the Good Friday Agreement to form the 'Real IRA' and the 'Continuity IRA'.

←**Source D**
Republican mural on Falls Road, Belfast (1988).

↑ **Source E**
Loyalist mural on Roden Street, Belfast (1994). The mural shows a UFF (Loyalist paramilitary) man. The quote was originally used in the Scots struggle against the English in 1320 and the muralists have redefined the target as the Irish.

TASKS

1. Divide your page into two sections headed 'Evidence of obstacles to peace' and 'Evidence of progress towards peace'. Ensure plenty of space as you will add to this throughout this case study. Using the sources, write down evidence that could be put into each section. For example: Obstacles to peace: The 'Real IRA' bombed Omagh, killing 29 people. Progress to peace: Politicians across the communities rejected this return to violence.

2. Look closely at the murals (see Sources D and E). What message do you think these are meant to send?

3. Look at Source C. What patterns do you see about the links between religious identity and national identity? Do you think this makes it more or less likely to achieve peace in Northern Ireland?

Timeline – The Troubles

1968 Civil rights campaign focused upon areas of perceived discrimination against Catholics: in council housing allocation; government jobs; policing (the Royal Ulster Constabulary and its reserve force the 'B' Specials were predominantly Protestant) and the 'gerrymandering' (rigging) of electoral boundaries to create Protestant majorities on local councils. Clashes at marches led to the announcement of reforms by the Stormont government (Northern Ireland government).

1969 Rioting followed a Loyalist parade in Londonderry. British troops were sent in. The troops were initially welcomed by the Catholics but soon the army was seen as the enemy by the Republicans.

1971 'Internment' was introduced, which gave the police power to arrest and detain anyone suspected of terrorist offences. This continued until 1975. Civil rights protests followed.

Bloody Sunday

1972 30 January 'Bloody Sunday' – 13 people were shot dead (plus another man died of his injuries later) when British troops opened fire on a civil rights march in Londonderry. The army claimed that its men were under attack from gunfire and nail bombs from the crowd, but no bombs or guns were recovered. The subsequent 'Widgery Tribunal' concluded that the army had been fired upon but that the dead had been unarmed. Nationalists were angry over this conclusion.

1972 March – 'Direct Rule' was announced by the British Prime Minister. Northern Ireland was to be governed directly from Westminster. More troops were sent in.

1973 An attempt was made to create a new 'power-sharing' Northern Ireland Assembly. It also proposed a 'Council of Ireland' to discuss issues affecting the North and South of Ireland. Unionists were split over these ideas.

1974 The Ulster Workers Council (Protestant Trade Unionists) strike against 'power sharing'.

Source F

"Before Bloody Sunday, I believe there were no more than 30–40 IRA volunteers in Derry. They had a very small base, small amounts of hardware and, most importantly, very little support ... we were still reasonably integrated in the city. The IRA's campaign of violence that followed in the wake of Bloody Sunday ... changed all that."

One of the founders of the SDLP recalls Bloody Sunday.

1976 The British government announced that those convicted of political offences would be treated as criminals. IRA prisoners in the Maze prison protested.

1976 The 'Peace People' began, following the deaths of three young children in the Troubles. Initially the campaign attracted mass support in demanding an end to violence.

Source G

"When Bobby Sands died, many of us felt that it's back to square one. If you tried to call a peace rally now you wouldn't get anyone to come."

Mairead Corrigan, leader of the 'Peace People' (December 1981)

1981 IRA prisoners in the Maze went on 'hunger strikes' over the loss of 'political' status. Their leader, Bobby Sands, died in May. 100 000 people turned out on the streets of Belfast for his funeral.

1984 The Anglo-Irish Agreement was signed by the British and Irish governments. The Republic of Ireland got some say in policy in Northern Ireland; the Republic accepted that Unionist agreement would be needed for a united Ireland. Unionist marches attacked this 'betrayal'. Republicans were angry that Ireland had, in effect, recognised partition.

1987 An IRA bomb killed 11 people at a Remembrance Day ceremony in Enniskillen.

1993 The Downing Street Declaration was made by the British and Irish governments. Both agreed to involve those parties committed to peaceful methods in forming a 'new political framework based upon consent'.

1994 IRA ceasefire, shortly followed by a Loyalist ceasefire. American Senator George Mitchell was called in to propose a way forward on key issues, such as the 'decommissioning' of weapons.

1996 IRA ceasefire ends with the bombing of Canary Wharf, London.

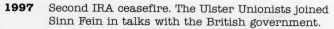

1997 Second IRA ceasefire. The Ulster Unionists joined Sinn Fein in talks with the British government.

1998 Good Friday Agreement was reached. Its main terms were:
- A united Ireland could not happen without the consent of the majority in Northern Ireland.
- The Republic of Ireland removed its claim to Northern Ireland from its constitution.
- A new Assembly was to be created to rule Northern Ireland.
- The Royal Ulster Constabulary (RUC) was to be reformed.
- The release of paramilitary prisoners.
- All parties to work together on decommissioning.
- A referendum on the agreement was to be held in both the North and the South of Ireland.

The Orange Parade

1999 The tragedy of the Omagh bombing. Further talks were held between the main political parties, but mistrust grew because of:
- Loyalist anger over the ban of the Orange Parade in Drumcree. Catholics living on the route felt that the march was intimidating.

Unionists felt that they had a right to march and to keep their traditions.
- Unionists were suspicious over the delay in IRA decommissioning of weapons.

2000 Further breakdowns in the process of decommissioning led to the re-introduction of 'direct rule'. In May, the Assembly was brought back following an IRA agreement to inspection of its weapons by international observers.

2001 At the general election, there were gains for the Democratic Unionists and for Sinn Fein. Conflict rose, as clashes between residents on the Ardoyne estate broke out. In October the IRA declared that the process of putting its weapons 'beyond use' had begun. This was confirmed by international observers. The Assembly Executive was re-established with David Trimble as First Minister.

Source H

Unemployment statistics for Protestants and Catholics 1971–1991.

Men			
	A Protestant	**B Catholic**	**Ratio A:B**
1971	6.5%	17.3%	2:6
1981	12.4%	30.25%	2:4
1991	12.7%	28.4%	2:2

Women			
	A Protestant	**B Catholic**	**Ratio A:B**
1971	3.6%	7.0 %	1:9
1981	9.6%	17.1%	1:8
1991	8.0%	14.5%	1:8

Source: Standing Advisory Committee on Human Rights

TASKS

1. Using the Timeline and the sources, identify the methods used to end conflict in Northern Ireland. Add this to your evidence of progress towards peace.

2. Using the Timeline and the sources, identify the issues and events that have increased tensions. Add this to the evidence of obstacles to peace.

3. Look at Source H. One complaint by nationalists was that religious/political identity affected your job prospects. Does this source seem to support this interpretation? Has the situation improved or deteriorated? What other evidence would you require in order to reach a firm condition?

4. The annual marching season in Northern Ireland often raises tensions. How would you argue for and against allowing one group to march, if it is seen as intimidatory to another group because of conflicting identities? Consider the implications for freedoms and rights. Are there other examples of this dilemma within the UK?

5. Look closely at the terms of the Good Friday Agreement and read again the views of political groups on page 21. Some Unionists and some Republicans have rejected this Agreement. Why do you think they have done this?

Steps backwards and steps forwards?

You have examined some of the past key events and issues of the Troubles and have identified some of the difficulties in ending conflict. In this section you will be looking at additional evidence which helps to explain why conflict has been hard to resolve and how groups are trying to create peace.

Steps backwards

1. The legacy for the young

Young people are disproportionately killed as a result of the Troubles. Almost 6% of those killed between 1969–1998 were aged 12–17, and the figures are even higher for those aged 18–24. Half the young people in a 2000 survey had been caught up in rioting and nearly 17% had witnessed a shooting. A third had seen someone killed or seriously injured. 45% felt endangered if they strayed into the 'wrong area'. A fifth said that friendships and relationships had ended or been affected because of sectarian division.

This experience suggests that sectarian identity is reinforced at a young age, making peace more difficult to maintain. It has also left a legacy of bitterness and mistrust. Some have argued that the number of church schools (schools which serve a particular religious denomination) does not contribute to an integrated society.

Source I

Results of a survey conducted in 2001. 1000 people were polled in Northern Ireland and 1000 in the Republic of Ireland. The survey looked at the levels of respect for culture and traditions.

- 32% of Catholics believed that respect between the two communities had increased.
- 11% of Catholics felt that respect between the two communities had decreased.
- 23% of Protestants felt that respect between the two communities had increased.
- 21% of Protestants felt that it had decreased.
- 32% of Protestants felt that there were aspects of their cultural traditions that were intimidating or threatening; 27% of Catholic respondents felt this way about their cultural traditions.
- 86% of Catholics answered that they had respect for the cultural traditions of Protestants and Unionists in Northern Ireland.
- 75% of Protestants said that they had respect for the cultural traditions of Catholics in Northern Ireland.

Source J

"Nearly 1000 people have been forced into exile since the signing of the Good Friday Agreement ... Those who dare to defy paramilitary orders are punished with death. Most experts argue that the attacks are the result of a breakdown in law and order caused by the Troubles. In Republican areas, the official police force, the RUC, has little credibility and members of the community turn to paramilitaries to 'get something done' about petty criminals."

From the 'Search for Peace' Report

2. Disaffection from the political process and lack of confidence in systems of justice

In 1969, the RUC had 3500 officers, 11% of whom were Catholic. At the time Nationalists felt that this meant the systems of law and order favoured the Unionist side. The RUC have argued that they have been fighting terrorists and that they have suffered as a result: 302 officers have been killed during the 30 years of the Troubles. Sinn Fein MPs did not take up their seats won in general elections because they did not recognise the legitimacy of Westminster, or the oath of allegiance to the Crown. Therefore, some would see a vote for Sinn Fein as a vote against the authority of Westminster.

3. The deep-rooted sectarian identity linked to economic problems

Some explanations point to the long history of mistrust and to the relative economic deprivation of some areas of Northern Ireland. This makes it likely that people will cling more closely to an identity which provides a network of support and a sense of worth. Competition for economic resources becomes more intense and concessions on cultural traditions less likely.

Steps forward

1. Cross-community projects with young people

Organisations such as 'Co-operation Ireland' run school exchange programmes between the North and South. They run a 'Civic Link' programme which asks students to pick one feature of their local area for improvement and to work co-operatively on improving it. The Youth Council for Northern Ireland identifies schemes like these as helpful in reducing the likelihood of sectarian bullying.

There is also increasing demand for places at integrated schools (schools which are not linked to one religious denomination) within Northern Ireland. In 2000, demand for places exceeded the number available by 1000. The school curriculum includes 'Education for Mutual Understanding', promoting respect for different cultures.

←Source K
A child holding a 'Yes' to referendum banner.

2. Economic growth

The EU has awarded grants to business in Northern Ireland on condition that the project creates across-community partnership. The Special Support Programme for Peace and Reconciliation was a response to the 1994 ceasefire and the boards which monitor the funds released by this EU initiative include representatives from across the community. The peace process has also improved the economic life of Northern Ireland (called the 'Peace Dividend'). In the 1990s, Ireland experienced rapid economic growth. Unemployment fell from 17.2% in 1986 to 6.2% in 2001. The increased confidence saw a 40% rise in house prices from 1996. There was increased overseas investment. Tourism also increased, with a 19% rise in visitors in 1999.

3. Political factors

The 1999 Patten Report recommended major changes to the police force of Northern Ireland in order to recruit from across the communities and to improve trust. These changes have been implemented in part. Sinn Fein MPs have been given office facilities at Westminster and have been excused taking the oath of allegiance in an attempt to make Westminster truly representative of the Northern Irish voters. The large majority who voted 'Yes' in the referendum on the Good Friday Agreement has been seen as a positive move towards peace.

The Saville Inquiry into the events of Bloody Sunday has also been welcomed by Nationalists as a step towards a full investigation of this event.

TASKS

1. Source J suggests that the police were not in control, or welcome, in some parts of Northern Ireland. Why would this be a problem in a democratic society? Why would it make it more difficult in creating peace?
2. You are presenting a research paper to the United Nations on conflict resolution: A case study of Northern Ireland. Use the two columns of evidence collected throughout this case study; you will need to choose some of the evidence to back up your points. Remember you may need an Introduction, discussion of the obstacles to peace and steps towards peace, and your view on which evidence is the most convincing.

GCSE CHECK

Demonstrate your knowledge and understanding of current issues

Show understanding of the importance of community identities and how these can come into conflict

Explain and interpret different kinds of information and analyse evidence in a variety of forms

Rights

Aim

This section focuses upon 'rights' and by the end of the three case studies you will:

- understand how civil and criminal law differ and how courts work
- consider who protects the rights of British citizens, refugees and those who have broken the law
- analyse the role of the media in forming opinions
- understand what is meant by the 'culture of rights and responsibility', and what being a good citizen involves.

A 'right' is something to which everyone is entitled. Broadly speaking, human rights fall into one of two types, and sometimes they can bridge both categories.

- On the one hand there are 'moral rights' – these are civil and political rights (or 'first generation' rights). For example, the right to life, to privacy, to protection from arbitrary arrest, to a fair trial, and to hold religious or political beliefs.
- The second group are 'legal rights' – these are economic, social and cultural rights (or 'second generation' rights). These include an adequate standard of living, education and health care, reasonable working conditions and commercial or consumer rights.

There is, of course, a big difference between the right to do something (rights) – and the right thing to do (responsibilities and duties). You have both rights **and** responsibilities.

In the UK a body of regulations passed by Parliament, called laws, protect your basic rights. Everyone is expected to conform to a common code of behaviour, including obedience to criminal and civil law (see Source A).

- Civil laws decide issues concerning property, taxation or child custody and are dealt with in a County or High Court.
- The police enforce criminal laws. A Magistrates Court deals with less serious criminal offences – such as speeding and vandalism – where penalties such as fines and probation orders can be given. The more serious offences – such as murder, fraud or kidnap – are usually dealt with by a Crown Court and prison sentences can be a punishment option.

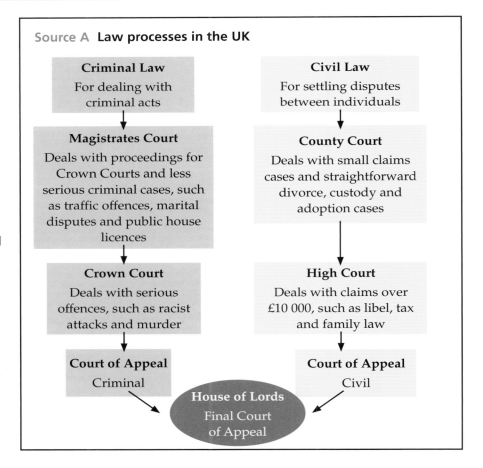

Source A **Law processes in the UK**

Criminal Law For dealing with criminal acts	**Civil Law** For settling disputes between individuals
Magistrates Court Deals with proceedings for Crown Courts and less serious criminal cases, such as traffic offences, marital disputes and public house licences	**County Court** Deals with small claims cases and straightforward divorce, custody and adoption cases
Crown Court Deals with serious offences, such as racist attacks and murder	**High Court** Deals with claims over £10 000, such as libel, tax and family law
Court of Appeal Criminal	**Court of Appeal** Civil

House of Lords Final Court of Appeal

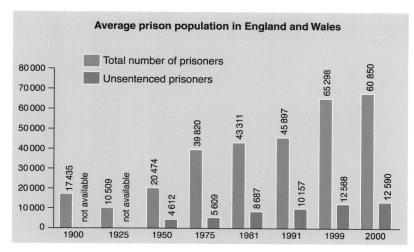

Average prison population in England and Wales

Total number of prisoners
Unsentenced prisoners

	1900	1925	1950	1975	1981	1991	1999	2000
Total number of prisoners	17 435	10 509	20 474	39 820	43 311	45 897	65 298	60 850
Unsentenced prisoners	not available	not available	4 612	5 609	8 687	10 157	12 568	12 590

TASK

Look carefully at Source B.

a) What reasons do you think there are for the large increase in prison sentences between 1991 and 1999?
b) Why do you think there was a drop in the number of prisoners between 1900 and 1925?

←Source B
Average prison population in England and Wales.

In both criminal and civil cases, a judge acts as a referee and interpreter of the law. In civil cases it is the plaintiff (the party making a claim) versus the defendant (the party against whom the claim is made) and the judge decides on the outcome of the case. In criminal cases, it is the prosecution versus the defence and the verdict is decided by a jury – a group of 12 electors chosen at random aged 18–65. If the jury passes a guilty verdict the judge decides the sentence.

If found guilty, the defendant has the right to take their case to a Court of Appeal. A Court of Appeal has the authority to review and reverse the decision of a lower court. On appeal, no new evidence is introduced. The Court of Appeal considers whether the lower court made a mistake on a question of law or reached a decision contrary to the evidence presented during trial.

Not all countries recognise human rights in the same way as the UK, nor do they have what is seen as a fair justice system. As you read through the three case studies you will learn that, even in the UK, not all human rights are absolute.

In Case Study 1 you will see how the rights of British citizens are protected. In Case Studies 2 and 3 you will discover how people can be denied their basic human rights by the ruling authority of the country.

Throughout the world, one person in every 150 is a refugee or displaced person. Every day millions are forced to flee their homes because their lives are in danger. Most of these refugees settle in neighbouring poor countries, but a small number arrive in rich countries like the UK. They hope to be received warmly and sheltered in safety. As you shall see these hopes are not always realised. Despite having human rights – and through no fault of their own – they will face a difficult future.

TASKS

1. 'Only criminals should fear the law.' Do you agree?
2. Can you think of any laws that you disagree with? Should people obey laws that they disagree with?

TASK

'Imagine coming home from school and finding your parents missing and your home destroyed. Imagine arriving in a new country and not knowing a word of the language. This happens every day to refugees.'
In your opinion:
a) What rights should refugees be entitled to?
b) What responsibilities do we have towards those refugees who arrive in the UK?

↑ Source C
A never ending journey?

What rights do **British people** have as citizens?

Aim

You will:

- understand what rights British people have as citizens and explore the importance of human rights legislation
- gain an appreciation of the rights and responsibilities stemming from consumer and employment laws
- examine the debate regarding identity cards.

Citizenship implies that everybody has access to the same rights and is protected by the same laws. Some rights are results of custom and general agreement, whereas others are contained in written Acts of Parliament.

Four international agreements have an important bearing on human rights and fundamental freedoms in the UK.

1. The United Nations Universal Declaration of Human Rights 1948

In 1945, after the devastation of the Second World War, the General Assembly of the newly created United Nations set up an 18-member commission headed by the former American First Lady, Eleanor Roosevelt. The commission spent three years drafting the Universal Declaration of Human Rights (UNDHR) and it was adopted on 10 December 1948 (see Source A).

↑ **Source A**
Eleanor Roosevelt – 'She would rather light a candle than curse the darkness.'

2. The European Convention on Human Rights 1950

On 4 November 1950 more than 40 European countries signed the European Convention on Human Rights (ECHR). The European Commission of Human Rights was founded in 1954. Its task is to see that human rights are upheld in all the European Union (EU) countries. The European Court of Human Rights was set up in 1959 in Strasbourg, and allowed individuals with a complaint against their state to have their case heard at an international level. In reality this was an expensive and lengthy process. The Human Rights Act 1998 means that UK citizens can now go through British courts rather than Strasbourg.

Source B

"Where, after all, do universal human rights begin? In small places, close to home – so close and so small that they cannot be seen on any map of the world. Yet they are the world of the individual person."

Eleanor Roosevelt (1958)

What rights do British people have as citizens?

Two initiatives highlight the importance that British governments have attached to examining the rights of its citizens.

1. One Conservative government campaigned to promote 'active citizenship'. In other words, every British citizen had a duty to take an active part in solving society's problems. The Citizen's Charter was part of this and was launched in 1991. This emphasised the two aspects of citizenship:
   a) concern for the responsibilities of citizens towards each other
   b) what citizens should expect as a right from the state.

2. The Labour government elected in 1997 pledged their commitment to 'strengthen education for citizenship'. At the same time as promising to strengthen citizens' rights, the Labour government emphasised that citizens also have responsibilities and duties towards the state and each other. On 2 October 2000, The Human Rights Act came into force. It was described as the most important human rights reform of the last 50 years. Some people objected to many of the laws passed in the 1980s and early 1990s which resulted in British citizens losing some of their rights and liberties. Sometimes the authorities appear to overrule certain rights that we, as citizens, believe are important.

In May 2001, for example, many protesters at an anti-capitalist demonstration in London complained that they were being denied their right to peaceful public protest (see Source C).

3. The Maastricht Treaty 1993

Maastricht is officially known as the Treaty of the European Union and with it the EU came into existence for the first time. The people of the 12 member states were given European citizenship, allowing them to move and live in any EU state.

4. The Human Rights Act 2000

This Act incorporated the European Convention on Human Rights into UK law. What this meant in practice was that British citizens no longer had to spend years pursuing a lengthy and costly case at the European Court of Human Rights in Strasbourg. Now if someone believes their rights have been abused, they can apply directly to the British courts.

The Human Rights Act (HRA) mainly protects rights under three broad categories:

- Fundamental rights – for example, the right to life and the right not to be subjected to torture.
- Procedural rights – such as the right to a fair trial and a fair hearing.
- Qualified rights – such as freedom of expression, the right to a private and family life and the right to freedom of association.

TASKS

1. It was said that Eleanor Roosevelt preferred to 'light a candle than curse the darkness'. What do you think was meant by this comment?

2. Why do you think that the UNDHR and ECHR are so important? Can you think of reasons why they might affect you personally?

↑ **Source C**
Protestors at the May Day demonstration complained about the aggressive tactics of the police.

As a result of the HRA, British citizens have the following basic rights and liberties (see Source D).

When the Act was introduced the Home Secretary said it would "develop a culture of rights and responsibility". Being a good citizen involves being aware of problems, expressing concerns and trying to put right things that are believed to be wrong.

The importance attached to rights and responsibilities can be clearly seen in consumer and employment laws.

Consumer rights

There are certain basic legal rights you have when you buy goods or services. These rights apply to goods bought or hired from a shop, street market, mail order catalogue, doorstep seller or over the Internet. They include goods bought in sales. And when you pay for a service, the law entitles you to expect certain standards.

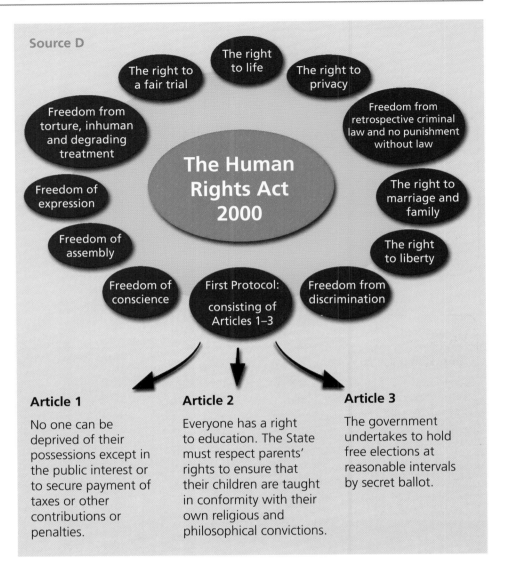

Source D

The Human Rights Act 2000

- The right to a fair trial
- The right to life
- The right to privacy
- Freedom from torture, inhuman and degrading treatment
- Freedom from retrospective criminal law and no punishment without law
- Freedom of expression
- The right to marriage and family
- Freedom of assembly
- The right to liberty
- Freedom of conscience
- First Protocol: consisting of Articles 1–3
- Freedom from discrimination

Article 1

No one can be deprived of their possessions except in the public interest or to secure payment of taxes or other contributions or penalties.

Article 2

Everyone has a right to education. The State must respect parents' rights to ensure that their children are taught in conformity with their own religious and philosophical convictions.

Article 3

The government undertakes to hold free elections at reasonable intervals by secret ballot.

What rights do you have as a consumer?

Well, first of all there is the **Sale of Goods Act 1979**.

Goods we buy must:

- be of satisfactory quality
- be free from defects (except when marked 'shop soiled')
- be fit for their purpose
- fit the description used in any advert, label or packaging.

The retailer has a legal obligation to sort out your problem if the goods do not meet these requirements.

There is also the **Consumer Protection Act 1987**. Anyone who sells you goods that are not safe is breaking the law. This applies to both new and second-hand products, but not to antiques. The Act also makes it an offence to mislead customers about the price of goods.

Then there is the **Supply of Goods and Services Act 1982** and **1994**. This states that you are entitled to certain standards when you pay for a service. A service should be carried out:

- with reasonable care and with a proper degree of skill
- within a reasonable time
- at a reasonable charge (if no price has been fixed in advance).

If something goes wrong as a result of the work done you can ask the contractor to put the work right.

Factfile

Employment rights

Any business has a duty to provide its employees with a safe working environment and must respect employees' rights. Important laws governing employment are:

- The Health and Safety at Work Act 1974 ensures safe and healthy working conditions.
- The Employment Protection (Consolidation) Act 1978 protects individuals from being unfairly dismissed.
- The Disability Discrimination Act 1995, the Race Relations Act 1976 and the Sex Discrimination Acts 1975 and 1986 make it unlawful to discriminate against individuals on the grounds of disability, sex, marital status, race, colour or ethnic or national origin.
- The Working Time Regulations Act 1998 covers areas such as maximum working hours, rest breaks and paid annual leave.
- The National Minimum Wage Act 1999 provides employees with basic protection from exploitation.

Several changes have been made to bring UK law in line with European legislation. In November 2001 the Employment Bill – effective from April 2003 – covered workplace disputes and maternity rights.

- Amount of paid and unpaid maternity leave was increased. Fathers were also given the right to two weeks' unpaid paternity leave. Most other European countries have more generous maternity rights.

TASKS

1. In your opinion, which three of the basic rights and liberties set out in Source D are the most important?
2. You have been asked to create a pamphlet that will help to inform people about their consumer rights. Try to find out about the following:
   a) Which laws are designed to protect the consumer?
   b) What rights does the consumer have regarding the buying and returning of goods?
   c) Are manufacturers' guarantees worth having?
   d) Are you obliged to accept a credit note?
   e) If you are dissatisfied, how do you go about making a complaint?

The identity card debate

The last time people in the UK were obliged to carry identity cards was during the Second World War. Identity cards were abolished in 1952. At the time, Lord Chief Justice Goddard said that the nation was no longer faced with a military threat, and that ID checks were actually obstructing the police rather than assisting them.

The terrorist acts which occurred in New York in September 2001 and the so-called 'invasion' of asylum seekers from continental Europe have renewed calls to reintroduce identity cards. In comparison to other countries, the UK is a relatively unpoliced society. In other European nations, both citizens and refugees must carry identity cards and present them to the authorities if requested. Some politicians suggested that because the UK does not insist on people carrying proof of identity, this was one reason why asylum seekers cross Europe to reach the UK.

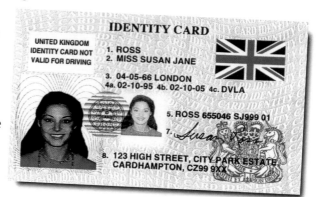

Advances in technology mean that an identity card could now incorporate features that would be much harder to forge. It could, for example, include:

- Automatic fingerprint recognition – police could verify a person's identity by swiping the thermal image of the cardholder's fingerprint.
- Iris recognition – when the card is swiped it could recognise the unique pattern on your iris.

Source E
In a recent MORI Poll individuals were asked the following questions about the use of identity cards and what features they felt should be included on them.

Q1 On balance, do you support or oppose the government introducing a national identity card scheme?

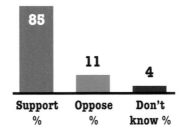

Support % · Oppose % · Don't know %
85 · 11 · 4

Do you think the introduction of identity cards would be successful or unsuccessful …

Q2 … in helping the Police tackle crime?
Q3 … in helping prevent terrorist attacks?
Q4 … in identifying those who are in the country illegally?

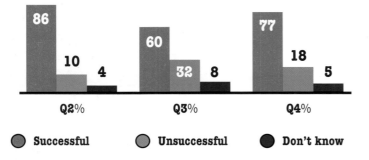

Q2%: 86 · 10 · 4
Q3%: 60 · 32 · 8
Q4%: 77 · 18 · 5

● Successful ● Unsuccessful ● Don't know

Q5 If the government did introduce a card, please tell me whether you would be willing or not for each of these pieces of information to be stored on it?

	Willing%	Not willing%	Don't know%
Date of birth	96	3	1
Photograph	97	3	0
Eye colour	92	7	1
Fingerprint	85	14	1
DNA details	75	21	4
Religion	67	31	2
Criminal records	74	23	3

Source: MORI/News of the World

TASK

1. Read through the information provided on this page. Discuss what features and information you think are essential for an identity card. Should it include:
   - DNA?
   - blood group?
   - whether the bearer wants to donate organs?
   - criminal records?
   - relevant immigration status?
   - religion?

I don't like the idea of the police having the power to stop you and demand to see your identity card. As for combatting illegal immigration, I think there is a risk that it could cause racial harassment and set back good race relations. ID cards might have advantages but what if they are used for something far more sinister?

Lots of people are asked to present driving licences, credit cards and work IDs. In 2001, an opinion poll taken soon after the terrorist attacks on the New York World Trade Center showed that 86% of people were in favour of some form of ID card. What have innocent people got to fear? I think that they would help the police in tracing suspects, combatting credit card fraud and other crimes involving stolen identities.

←Source F
Armed police make a security check … some officers believe identity cards would be a valuable help in the fight against crime.

TASK

"What did you do for others? This is the breadth of life. … We must learn that there is nothing greater than to do something for others."

Dr Martin Luther King Jnr. (1967)

Having read this section and undertaken some of the activities, how far do you think individuals should be more concerned with responsibilities rather than rights?

GCSE CHECK

| International agreements protect basic human rights of individuals | The rights and responsibilities of consumers, employers and employees | European legislation has an effect on legal decisions in the UK | Develop skills of questionnaire use and statistics/data analysis |

How should refugees and asylum seekers be treated?

Aim

You will:

- understand the definitions of Refugees, Asylum seekers and IDPs and the work of the UNHCR
- begin to understand why people become refugees and what life is like for many of them
- understand the legal context of how asylum seekers are treated in the UK and what their rights are
- explore popular and media 'myths' about asylum seekers.

More people than ever before are fleeing from war, persecution or disaster. Worldwide, over 20 million people are refugees. As you work through this case study you will discover that there can be many reasons for being a refugee such as: civil unrest, war, forced relocation and famine and drought. Under international law, the word 'refugee' has a very precise meaning, as set out in the 1951 United Nations Convention Relating to Refugees. In the Convention, a refugee is defined as someone who:

- has a well-founded fear of persecution for reasons of race, religion, nationality, membership of a particular social group, or political opinion;
- is outside the country they belong to or normally reside in, and
- is unable or unwilling to return home for fear of persecution.

In poor countries refugee status is usually given automatically. Refugee status gives individuals legal protection and help with food, clothing and water. The legal term 'asylum seeker' – only used in developed countries – refers to a refugee who is seeking permission to settle in a new country. To gain residential rights, asylum seekers need to prove that they have 'a well-founded fear of persecution'. People who are looking for a better life are classed as 'economic refugees'. This is not usually a reason to be granted asylum. A further term is Internally Displaced Persons (IDPs). These people (an estimated 25 million) have been forced to flee their homes, but have not reached a neighbouring country. Therefore, unlike refugees or asylum seekers, they are not protected by international law or eligible to receive many types of aid.

↓ Source A

Map showing routes of world refugee movements. Many refugees come from war zones such as Palestine/Israel, Rwanda, Burundi, Eritrea, Sudan, Afghanistan, Bosnia, Iraq, Somalia, Sierra Leone, China, Kosovo, Angola, Congo, Indonesia, Columbia and Sri Lanka.

① Palestine	② Afghanistan	③ Bosnia	④ Iraq	⑤ Somalia	⑥ Sierra Leone
⑦ China	⑧ Sri Lanka	⑨ Kosovo	⑩ Angola	⑪ Congo	⑫ Sudan
⑬ Rwanda and Burundi	⑭ Eritrea	⑮ Indonesia	⑯ Colombia		

↑ Source B
The growing refugee problem.

The work of the United Nations High Commission for Refugees (UNHCR)

The largest refugee organisation in the world is the United Nations High Commission for Refugees. It was set up in 1951. Its headquarters are in Geneva, Switzerland, and it has offices in more than 120 countries. Its main purpose, often working with other agencies such as Oxfam and The Refugee Council, is to protect refugees and try to find permanent solutions to their problems.

UNHCR has four different jobs:
- To make sure that refugees are not sent back to places where their lives would be in danger.
- To see that all governments treat refugees fairly.
- To work with other organisations to make sure that aid reaches refugees.
- To solve refugees' long-term problems, UNHCR tries to help people return home if it becomes safe for them to do so. If this is impossible, it helps them to settle in a new country.

The UNHCR helps provide protection and assistance not only to refugees, but also to other types of displaced or needy persons. These include asylum seekers, refugees who have returned home but still need help in rebuilding their lives, local communities that are directly affected by the movements of refugees and, perhaps most importantly, growing numbers of internally displaced persons (IDPs).

Most countries are members of the United Nations, which was set up shortly after the end of the Second World War. Its aim is to promote peace, justice and a better life for all the people of the world. In 1948 it produced the Universal Declaration of Human Rights. The right to seek refuge from persecution or war is one of the clear articles of the Declaration.

With international travel and increasing numbers of refugees and people seeking asylum, some countries – including the UK – have toughened their asylum procedures.

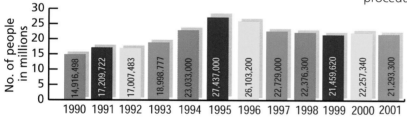

↑ Source C
Annual totals worldwide of persons of concern to UNHCR.

↓ Source D
Origin of major refugee populations in 2000.

Country of origin	Main countries of asylum	Refugees
Afghanistan	Pakistan, Iran	3 580 400
Burundi	Tanzania	568 000
Iraq	Iran	512 800
Sudan	Uganda, Congo, Ethiopia, Kenya, Chad	490 400
Bosnia-Herzegovina	Yugoslavia, Croatia, USA, Sweden, Netherlands, Denmark	478 300
Somalia	Kenya, Ethiopia, Yemen, Djibouti	447 800
Angola	Zambia, Congo, Namibia	432 700
Sierra Leone	Guinea, Liberia	400 800
Eritrea	Sudan	376 400
Vietnam	China, USA	370 300

TASKS

1. In your opinion, what is the basic difference between an 'asylum seeker' and a 'refugee'? What is an IDP?
2. Describe in your own words what the UNHCR is and what it does.
3. Study the information set out in Sources C & D. You have to write an article for a magazine's 'In My Opinion' column, examining why the number of refugees seeking asylum in European countries is small in comparison with the numbers of refugees that have to be dealt with in other parts of the world.
4. What do you think the more developed countries should be doing to help refugees?

Source E

Journey from Liberia – Marlboro's story

(Adapted from the BBC News World Road to Refuge)

Marlboro was a university graduate with a good job and his whole life ahead of him when civil war broke out in Liberia. There was chaos as people were killed or tried to flee to neighbouring countries.

He escaped to the Ivory Coast by foot, and then made his way to Lebanon. By this time, he learned that his mother and brother were dead. In Lebanon, he walked for three days across the mountains to Syria, where he met up with some men who, for £3500, agreed to smuggle him to Germany.

Marlboro knew little about the people who drove him and three other Africans to Europe with false papers. He never arrived in Germany. Instead, the smugglers abandoned the four men in Slovakia. By the time they realised they were not in Germany, the smugglers had disappeared – along with their passports.

Marlboro took a philosophical attitude to his experience of smuggling, which he likened to a business deal. "They took my money, but I got to the promised land," he said. "I was lucky. Others, they take their money, but they don't go anywhere."

In Slovakia, he obtained refugee status. His salary of £130 a month, however, was not enough to live on. In trying to fund a return trip to Africa, he moved again – this time to an EU country. As he had already been given asylum in Slovakia, he was forced to enter as an illegal immigrant. The only job he could find was washing dishes.

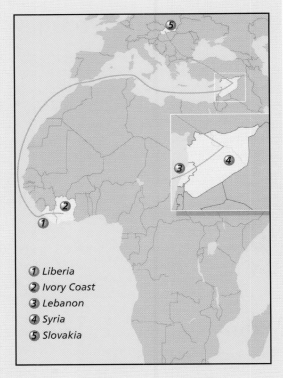

① Liberia
② Ivory Coast
③ Lebanon
④ Syria
⑤ Slovakia

If the law gave him freedom of movement in Western Europe, he could be more usefully employed. But, despite the terrible problems, he escaped from in Liberia, he has been forced into an underground world. As for his future, every day he lives in fear of being caught and possibly imprisoned.

Life as a refugee

The richer nations of Europe and North America are increasingly reluctant to take in refugees. Even countries like Tanzania, traditionally helpful towards refugees, are overwhelmed by the number of refugees coming to them. Most of them are women and children and they are fleeing from war zones or natural disasters (see Source F). The cost of supporting so many refugees is high, since land, shelter, food and water all have to be found.

Life in many of the refugee camps in these countries is grim. The refugees live in slum areas. Very few of them have passports and almost none of them have ID cards, without which they are often forbidden to work. What work they do find pays very poorly.

Even officially-recognised refugees sometimes do not receive adequate protection and assistance. IDPs are in a worse situation because they do not even get the same rights as refugees. In a country where there is a civil war, there may not be any well-organised camps to receive IDPs.

↑ **Source F**
Refugees fleeing to Tanzania.

Case Study 2

Source G
Refugees can be any age.

Basic services may have been destroyed, and fighting may make it difficult for aid organisations to provide relief. The reality is that the poor countries of the world provide protection to most refugees. Only a small percentage of 'displaced' people ask for asylum in the UK.

In 2000, 10 000 asylum seekers were given refugee status in the UK but over 40 000 people applied for asylum. Almost every week, stories concerning asylum seekers appear in the press, often revealing the desperate lengths some refugees go to in the hope of starting a new life in another country.

Asylum in the UK

The 2002 Nationality, Immigration and Asylum Bill and before this the 1999 Immigration and Asylum Act cover issues such as:

- entry into the UK
- the detention of asylum seekers and their dispersal around the country
- provision of financial support
- handling of their cases.

↓ **Source H**
Yarlswood Detention Centre, following a fire in 2002. Europe's largest detention centre, it had been the scene of numerous protests about living conditions for detainees since opening in late 2001.

Human rights organisations argued that the Government's systems for dealing with applications were in many ways unfair. They criticised unfair measures for detained people, a denial of access to mainstream education for children in accommodation centres, limited availability of legal advice and inequality of financial support (roughly 30% less than that for non-asylum-seekers receiving income support). Police groups have warned that negative reporting of asylum seekers and refugees can lead to racial hatred. In April 2002, the Home Secretary, David Blunkett, upset many groups fighting for the fair treatement of asylum seekers when he said that refugees were 'swamping' British schools.

TASKS

1. Role-play a scene where a journalist interviews a person living in a refugee camp. Before you begin, draw up a list of questions to ask. For example, What is life like in the camp? What are their hopes for the future?

2. 'In cases where people are economic refugees rather than refugees from political or religious persecution, it is right to return them to their own country.' Do you agree? Justify your answer.

Myths and realities

Britain is a soft touch and takes more than its fair share of refugees.

It is mainly the world's poorest countries such as Iran, Pakistan and Tanzania that bear the greatest 'asylum strain'. The vast majority of refugees go to neighbouring countries. If you compare numbers of refugees with the host country's national wealth (GDP), the UK ranks seventy-eighth in the world, and only eighth in Europe. Very restrictive immigration and asylum policies make it almost impossible for refugees to enter the UK legally, so many are forced into the hands of criminal traffickers.

Only a tiny proportion of refugees are genuine and the rest are 'bogus'.

The UK has to ensure that no one is forcibly returned to any country where their life or freedom may be in danger. Official figures show that around half of all asylum seekers need protection and are granted refugee status. Some, however, appear to be rejected unfairly: they may be turned down for entering the UK with false papers, despite the fact that this may have been the only way to escape persecution in their home country.

Asylum seekers get massive state handouts.

The UK gives asylum seekers less financial support than other European countries. The 1999 Act replaced cash benefits with a voucher scheme which was worth between 70–80% of income support levels. After much criticism, in October 2001, the Home Secretary announced that this scheme would be phased out. Asylum seekers are amongst the poorest and most vulnerable groups in the UK.

Most asylum seekers come from safe countries.

The majority of refugees come from countries where there have been serious conflicts and/or abuse of human rights. Some supposedly 'safe' European countries may not be as safe as we think because they all have different interpretations of who should be given refugee status. For example, France has a record of returning many Algerians home and Germany has returned Tamils to Sri Lanka. Both Tamils and Algerians have faced great dangers in being returned 'home'.

Council tax is going up to fund asylum seekers.

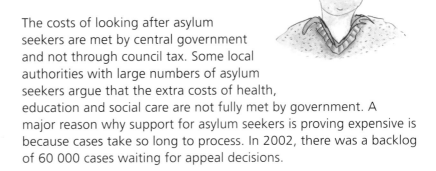

The costs of looking after asylum seekers are met by central government and not through council tax. Some local authorities with large numbers of asylum seekers argue that the extra costs of health, education and social care are not fully met by government. A major reason why support for asylum seekers is proving expensive is because cases take so long to process. In 2002, there was a backlog of 60 000 cases waiting for appeal decisions.

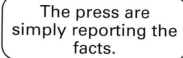

Refugees are begging aggressively and turning to crime.

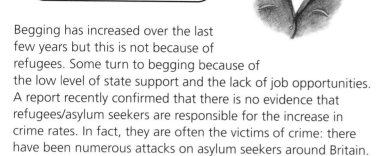

Begging has increased over the last few years but this is not because of refugees. Some turn to begging because of the low level of state support and the lack of job opportunities. A report recently confirmed that there is no evidence that refugees/asylum seekers are responsible for the increase in crime rates. In fact, they are often the victims of crime: there have been numerous attacks on asylum seekers around Britain.

The press are simply reporting the facts.

On several occasions, the Press Complaints Commission has warned newspaper editors about 'the danger that inaccurate and misleading reporting may generate an atmosphere of fear and hostility which is not borne out by the facts'.

Asylum seekers are taking our housing and UK jobs.

Asylum seekers are often housed in 'hard to let' accommodation that people on council waiting lists do not want. Evidence is growing that asylum seekers are also being exploited by private landlords.

Refugees are legally unable to work while awaiting the outcome of their applications. Even when they can work, it is difficult for them to find anything suitable, due to language problems, lack of training, and no transport.

Asylum seekers should all be locked up and sent back home.

Britain has signed the 1951 UN Convention on Refugees, which means that anyone has the legal right to come here and claim asylum. The majority of asylum seekers are granted temporary admission pending an outcome of their claim.

The fact that asylum seekers are held in a network of centres appears to be a breach of international human rights law. In addition, since January 2002, all new asylum seekers were issued with ID cards (Applicant Registration Cards – ARC), which includes a photograph and fingerprint data. Initial applicants are placed in induction centres near Heathrow and Croydon. Some will then be placed in accommodation centres. Those dispersed or who continue to live in London will be required to go regularly to a reporting centre so that the authorities can keep track of them.

TASKS

Unfortunately, not all of the daily media coverage is balanced or truthful.

Read the following claims A–C and then look carefully at the information given to you on these pages. Under the title 'Nailing press myths about refugees' set out your responses to each headline.

Claim A "We resent the scroungers, beggars and crooks who are prepared to cross every country in Europe to reach our generous benefits system." (From *The Sun*, 7/3/01)

Claim B "Many will have undoubtedly been hoping to end up in Britain, the number one destination for asylum-seekers." (From *The Daily Telegraph*, 19/2/01)

Claim C "Thousands have already [come to Britain], bringing terror and violence to the streets of many English towns." (From *The Sunday People*, 4/3/01)

New British laws are designed to block the arrival of desperate asylum seekers. Estimates of the number of 'illegal immigrants' are difficult to establish. A Home Office report in February 2002 estimated there were already 'hundreds of thousands of illegal migrant workers in Britain', although the basis of this figure is unclear. It is also uncertain whether the figures are rising.

Despite the fact that those allowed to remain receive very limited state handouts and few comforts, some refugees are now taking great risks to enter a country illegally.

The man who fell to earth

The woman who first found him assumed he was a drunk who had tumbled over the railings and fallen asleep while staggering home. As she edged over for a closer look, she noticed that his limbs were grotesquely misshapen, and the pool of lumpy liquid in which he was lying was not vomit, but the man's brains.

The area was quickly screened off and police launched an immediate murder investigation. It soon emerged that a witness had seen the dead man a few minutes before his body was found. A workman at nearby Heathrow airport had glanced upwards to see him falling from the sky like a stone. The police soon pieced together the details of Mohammed Ayaz's long journey from a remote village in Northwest Pakistan to his final, sorry end in the car park of a DIY superstore in Richmond.

The day before, at Bahrain airport, the 21-year-old had broken through a security cordon and climbed into the wheelbay of a Boeing 777. The undercarriage compartment had no oxygen, no heating, no pressure and no way out. Ten minutes after take-off the wheelbay temperature was freezing. At 18 000 feet he would have begun to hallucinate from lack of oxygen. At 30 000 feet, the temperature was minus 56 degrees.

Ayaz was as good as dead from the moment his feet left the runway. As the plane approached Heathrow, the wheels were lowered, and the frozen body was tipped out into the early morning sky.

Source I
Stowaway Ayaz thought he was safe in the wheelbay of the jet, but it was probably only when the wheels left the ground that he realised how much trouble he was in.

How should refugees and asylum seekers be treated?

↑ Source J
The container in which 58 Chinese asylum seekers were found dead.

Often we read stories of similar acts of desperation:

- A young Kosovan asylum seeker drowned after throwing himself from a cross-Channel ferry to avoid being sent back to Europe.
- In June 2000, the dead bodies of 58 Chinese asylum seekers were found by shocked Customs officials in the back of a truck arriving by cross-Channel ferry at Dover.
- In another incident in 2001, hundreds of illegal immigrants tried to break out of an asylum centre at Sangatte, France, to board Channel Tunnel trains into Britain. There were repeated calls from the British government and Eurotunnel to shut the centre and in May 2002 the French government confirmed it would close down.

Amid fears that Europe's refugee crisis became more unmanageable, the British Home Secretary promised tougher controls at Channel ports and fresh international efforts to curb asylum seekers.

Despite the truth, media coverage of asylum seekers often paints a picture of 'scroungers' coming to live on benefits and beg on the streets. In fact, government statistics show that people born outside the UK, including asylum seekers, contribute 10% more to the UK economy in taxes and national insurance than they consume in benefits and public services – equivalent to a boost to the economy of £2.6 billion.

According to OXFAM the core question for governments should be: 'How do we ensure that we recognise those in need of protection from persecution, and offer them a life in this country that offers them both security and a regard for their human rights?'

In contrast, what people seeking refugee status sometimes find on arrival in the UK is punishment for their misfortune, through the effects of some government policies and media misinformation.

TASKS

1. Do you agree with tougher controls for all asylum seekers? Should asylum seekers always be entitled to the right of appeal if their application to live in a country is turned down? Give reasons for your views.
2. Study the information in this unit.
   a. Why do people become refugees?
   b. Why do you think over 80% of refugees are women and children?
   c. How would you feel as a young person coming to the UK, escaping from a civil war or persecution? What sort of a life can you expect to lead in the UK as an asylum seeker?

GCSE CHECK

| Legal and human rights underpinning society | Origins of diverse identities in the UK | Need for mutual respect and understanding | Media's role in society | UK relations in Europe | Consider other people's experiences |

The criminal justice system
– is it **tough** enough**?**

Aim

You will:

- develop an understanding of the role and operation of the criminal justice system
- consider how some organisations work to protect the rights of those who find themselves on the wrong side of the law
- examine the debate regarding policing methods and the alternatives that are offered to imprisonment.

Crime, as portrayed in many television shows and films, is often shown as a glamorous, exciting business. 'Victimless crime' such as a clever fraud is almost applauded. In reality there is no such thing as a 'victimless crime'. People from both sides of the law suffer – from the prostitutes, illegal immigrants and drug addicts, to the victims of burglary, car crime and muggings.

Every year, we are told that crime rates are falling but figures can be misleading. Critics point out that 'new types of crime' such as Internet fraud and stalking do not show up in the figures. In addition, a huge number of crimes still go unreported.

Is the criminal justice system tough enough on offenders? Some criminals receive only light sentences and government ministers are becoming increasingly concerned with the 'revolving door syndrome'. As many as 75% of those convicted of burglary or theft re-offend within two years of being released.

Others believe that imprisonment should only be used as a last resort for violent offenders who pose a threat to society. They feel that resources should target crime prevention such as more policing, use of Closed Circuit Television (CCTV) systems and Neighbourhood Watch schemes.

Apart from Portugal, the UK sends more people to prison than any other Western European country. We imprison 125 people per 100 000 of the population. Prison is an expensive option – it costs over £500 per week to keep someone in prison. For the cost of a new prison we could build two hospitals or 60 primary schools.

↑ Source A
In recent years the crime rate in England and Wales has fallen. Yet more than one in four adults is a victim of crime.

Source B

"We see people that don't ever want to go to the police, people that will never ever be included in these statistics."

Victim Support

"People will admit to having been victims of burglary – but they're not going to admit to being beaten by a husband."

Professor Jock Young, Head of Criminology at Middlesex University

Factfile

In the UK, two groups are particularly committed to changing the criminal justice system: The Howard League For Penal Reform and the National Association for the Care and Resettlement of Offenders (NACRO).

The Howard League For Penal Reform

A leading prison reformer, John Howard, founded the organisation in 1866. It is entirely funded by voluntary donations. In trying to reform the penal system, it researches and comments on criminal justice policy and practice. It holds conferences and debates, publishes books and reports and also runs projects in schools and prisons.

NACRO

NACRO is an independent voluntary organisation trying to find practical solutions to reduce crime. It works with ex-offenders, disadvantaged people and deprived communities, helping them to build a better future. Its main aims are:

- resettling or housing people
- getting people into work
- working with young people
- finding better ways to reduce crime.

At times the justice system seems to be unable to cope with the changing face of crime and technology, trying to play 'catch-up' in areas such as cybercrime and electronic tagging. It faces difficult challenges from under-funding, the growth in the female prison population and the growing number of young offenders.

TASKS

1. Look closely at Source B – why should we treat crime statistics carefully? Suggest two reasons why some crimes are not reported.
2. In Source C, what is meant by the term 'institutionalised racism'?
3. Think about how prison is represented in films, TV soaps, books – are children featured?
4. Investigate the figures for crime and punishment in the UK over the last five years. Look at the website of the Office for National Statistics www.statistics.gov.uk, or the British Crime Survey www.homeoffice.gov.uk.
   a) What trends can you identify? Which crimes seem to be declining? Which ones are rising in number?
   b) Which crimes receive the heaviest sentences?

Source C

Who are we locking up?

- Since 1992 the prison population has increased by 43%. Nearly 95% of the inmates are male. In 2000, there were 67 800 people (roughly 0.1% of the UK population) in prison in England and Wales. By March 2002 this figure had risen to a record 70 019. The government says that the maximum number of inmates which can be safely held in prison is 71 000.
- 10 526 were young male offenders aged between 15–21.
- 564 were young female offenders aged between 15–21.

According to Home Office figures for 2002:

- 7% of prisoners were serving sentences of less than six months; 7% were serving sentences of six to 12 months; 38% were serving sentences of 12 months to less than four years; 39% were serving sentences of four years and over, excluding life prisoners; 9% were serving life sentences – of these 4840 were men, 160 were women and 160 were young people aged between 15–21.
- 77% of people committed to custody had committed non-violent crimes.
- 78% of prisoners were white, 15% black, 3% Asian and 4% Chinese and other.
- Over 22% of the prison population comes from ethnic minorities and yet only 6% of the general population is of ethnic origin. The rate of imprisonment per 100 000 of the population is 1265 for black people compared to 184 for white people. Many pressure groups feel that this 'institutionalised racism' cannot be tolerated.

Miscarriages of justice in the UK

The justice system faces criticism from all areas of society including the media, politicians, judiciary, police and pressure groups. There is heated debate in controversial areas such as arming police, electronic tagging, 'soft-option' sentencing, rehabilitation, curfews and dealing with the 'yob culture'. If all these aspects are not difficult enough to cope with, in recent years there have been outcries from the media and pressure groups about gross miscarriages of justice.

In the last 15 years many miscarriages of justice have surfaced. To avoid this in the future, groups like the Howard League for Penal Reform and NACRO believe we need to radically reform the criminal justice system. In the 1980s there was a series of well-publicised cases of 'miscarriages of justice'. Two cases in particular involved IRA bombing campaigns, the Birmingham Six (see Source E) and the Guildford Four.

The Birmingham Six

In this case, the police were accused of rounding up suspects and using false evidence to get convictions. In 1989, thanks to a television documentary team, the Court of Appeal released the Birmingham Six. More miscarriages of justice have since come to light. To help to investigate these cases an independent body – the Criminal Cases Review Commission (CCRC) – has been set up. The CCRC has a good track record. Over 73% of cases that have been referred back to the Court of Appeal by the CCRC have resulted in quashed convictions. The problem is that the CCRC is understaffed and it already has a backlog of 1200 cases (about one-third of all applications to date).

Since 1984 two pieces of legislation have also been introduced in an attempt to prevent further miscarriages of justice:

- The Police and Criminal Evidence Act (PACE) gives the police strict guidelines on how long they can question suspects for. All interviews are taped to ensure there is no unlawful pressure put on the suspect.
- The Criminal Procedure and Investigations Act aims to ensure that the Police or the Crown Prosecution Service (CPS) discloses to the defence everything which could be relevant to their case.

Recent surveys (see Source D), however, suggest that people are still not convinced about the 'justice' of the UK legal system.

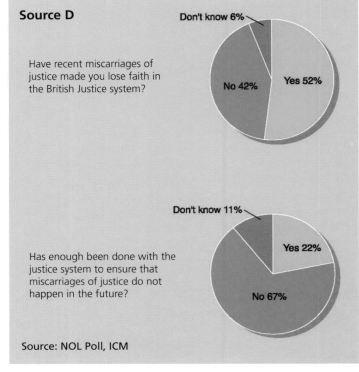

Source D

Have recent miscarriages of justice made you lose faith in the British Justice system?

Don't know 6%
No 42%
Yes 52%

Has enough been done with the justice system to ensure that miscarriages of justice do not happen in the future?

Don't know 11%
Yes 22%
No 67%

Source: NOL Poll, ICM

→ **Source E**
The release of the Birmingham Six in 1989 made world headlines.

The criminal justice system – is it tough enough?

Sometimes public opinion is very divided on the sentences passed in certain cases. In April 2000, a farmer, Tony Martin, was jailed for life for shooting a teenage burglar in the back who broke into his isolated farmhouse. He appealed and in October 2001 the charge was reduced from murder to manslaughter. In an interview Martin explained why he did it. "Look, I don't agree with shooting people. It's not something I take lightly. On the night of the burglary I was a terrified man alone in the house. ... I heard this murmuring and had this light shone in my eyes. All these things happened in a flash. I couldn't stand it any longer and then I just let the gun off."

Martin was known as a loner, and his views on crime were well-known. He told friends that he was prepared to defend his property against intruders, and he opened fire on the burglars with an illegally-held pump action shotgun. Martin suffered sexual abuse as a child and had a history of gun-related misbehaviour, dating back more than 20 years.

In January 2001 it was announced that the two children convicted of killing toddler James Bulger, were going to be allowed to go free with new identities. In 1993, when they were aged only ten, they abducted two-year-old James and battered him to death. James' mother stated, "The judge has slapped me in the face. ... The murderers have walked away to a life of luxury, a bought home, a bank account and 24-hour-protection."

Echoing many people's thoughts she also added, "They [the killers] will be recognised and found out under any new name wherever they go. Every minute they will have to look over their shoulders ... they will never be able to relax … they will always be haunted and hunted."

Her former husband – James's father – appealed for 'restraint' and 'time to reflect' after the release of his son's killers, concerned that innocent people could be caught up in any vigilante action to avenge his murdered son. While making it clear that he despised the two killers, he said: "I would not want another innocent family to suffer what we have been through. … But as a parent myself, the last thing I want is for innocent young men to be attacked, or worse, if they are mistaken for the boys who killed James."

Source F
James Bulger's grave.

TASK

You are an MP, and you have received these letters from your constituents. Read them through and write a response to each one.

Peter Church
14 Gordon Road, Perth
Scotland, PT5 7AB
Telephone 0453 784556

How can we stop violent crime if we constantly give in to these softies who defend the rights of the criminal while punishing the innocent? Tony Martin gets sent to prison for killing an intruder in self-defence while the two boys who killed James Bulger get just eight years. We seriously need to rethink our justice system.

Viv Leaman
76 Beatty Drive, Ashleigh,
Derbyshire, AS7 4CF
0145 733442
email vleaman@goweb.com

I see police holding speed cameras and pulling over drivers for driving 5mph over the limit. Yet every time there is a fight in a pub or someone is attacked or mugged in the street, where are the police officers? It's time the police got their priorities sorted out!

MARION BROMLEY
Peony Cottage, Thistle Lane, Healey,
Kent GL3 5DD. Tel & fax 0198 643367

Some criminals live better in prison than we do! Law-abiding citizens should not be paying for criminals to enjoy themselves in jail. Punishments need to punish and teach.

Yob culture

Excessive drinking is the cause of much of the violent behaviour portrayed so frequently in the media. Everyone knows what the term 'yob culture' means and it often comes up in the law and order debate. But who, and what, are we really talking about?

The usual suspects include the 'lager louts', soccer hooligans, and bored teenagers who hang out on street corners. While it may be identified with the young, yob culture is not confined to any one age group, or indeed one class. For example, many restaurant owners complain that some customers – including professionals like bankers and lawyers – indulge in drunken behaviour, and make racist and sexist remarks to waiters. Some people say it is just 'having a bit of fun', but should yobbish behaviour be accepted so easily?

Factfile

Alcohol and violence

- 40% of violent crime, 78% of assaults and 88% of criminal damage cases are committed while the offender is under the influence of alcohol.

- People who have been drinking commit 50%–80% of violent crime, including assault, rape and murder.

- Alcohol increases the tendency of male drinkers to be aggressive to others.

- Every year in the UK around 125 000 people suffer facial injuries as a result of violence. In many cases, either the victim or the assailant had been drinking alcohol. There are around 5000 'glassings' each year, where smashed beer glasses are used as dangerous weapons.

Source: The Home Office

Curfews

The 'yob culture' debate often focuses on how to deal with youngsters who are out on the streets at night, getting into trouble. One suggestion is to impose a night-time curfew on children under the age of 16. In areas with a reputation for juvenile crime and disorder, children would be banned from being out on certain streets after 9:00pm, unless they have adult supervision.

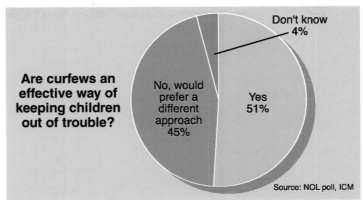

Are curfews an effective way of keeping children out of trouble?

Don't know 4%

No, would prefer a different approach 45%

Yes 51%

Source: NOL poll, ICM

Source H →

The problem is that local curfews are impossible to enforce, and may lead to resentment among young people who are not troublemakers. The head of NACRO's youth crime section, Chris Stanley believes, "It's unfair because it will penalise the law-abiding young who will have to stay at home. What's needed is a structured response that provides resources for young people. Youth clubs, sporting activities – these things would help get children off the streets, and prevent them getting into trouble."

Other proposals include authorising the police to impose fixed-penalty fines for acts of drunkenness and disorder, restrictions on drinking alcohol in certain public places, and the police could be given the power to close rowdy pubs and bars.

Rehabilitation

A familiar story is often heard throughout UK courts. Nearly half of those arrested across a whole range of crimes, from robbery and burglary, to shoplifting and prostitution, are trying to fund their drug habit. Sending someone to prison does not stop them getting hold of drugs. Once released, many drug-users quickly re-offend. Breaking the crime–drug link is one of the biggest challenges facing the criminal justice system today.

One solution to the problem is based on the successful drug court scheme in America. This is a criminal court that deals purely with offenders who have drug problems. If they undergo an intensive programme of treatment and rehabilitation they stay out of prison. Usually it lasts for at least a year and during that time offenders are regularly tested for drugs to make sure they remain clean. The court monitors their progress closely. Offenders know that if they do not stick to the programme, they will be imprisoned.

Putting more resources into areas like drug and alcohol rehabilitation seems to be a good investment because it reduces the chances of offenders returning to the courts. The trouble is that some politicians are worried about backing schemes that opponents claim are 'soft' on law-breakers.

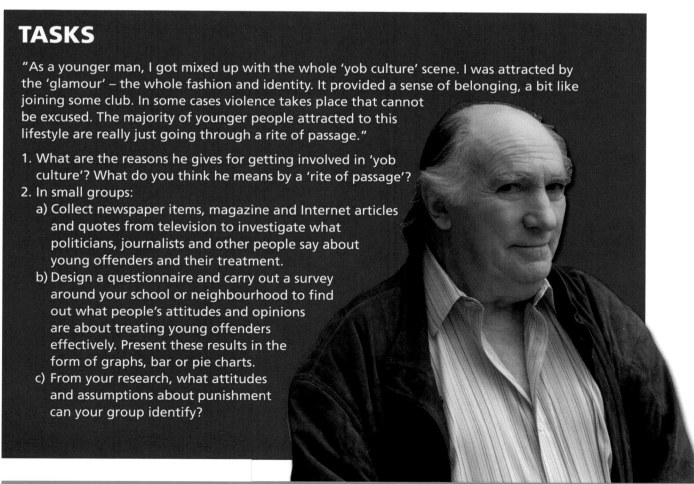

TASKS

"As a younger man, I got mixed up with the whole 'yob culture' scene. I was attracted by the 'glamour' – the whole fashion and identity. It provided a sense of belonging, a bit like joining some club. In some cases violence takes place that cannot be excused. The majority of younger people attracted to this lifestyle are really just going through a rite of passage."

1. What are the reasons he gives for getting involved in 'yob culture'? What do you think he means by a 'rite of passage'?
2. In small groups:
   a) Collect newspaper items, magazine and Internet articles and quotes from television to investigate what politicians, journalists and other people say about young offenders and their treatment.
   b) Design a questionnaire and carry out a survey around your school or neighbourhood to find out what people's attitudes and opinions are about treating young offenders effectively. Present these results in the form of graphs, bar or pie charts.
   c) From your research, what attitudes and assumptions about punishment can your group identify?

Electronic tagging

Imagine this scenario. Recently released from prison, a child sex offender has been warned to stay away from young people. One day, walking through his neighbourhood, he approaches a playground area. Within minutes, and before any crime has been committed, a police car pulls up and he is detained. His exact location is constantly tracked and a small transmitter sends a warning signal to the police that he is too close to potential victims.

Is this far-fetched? Not any more as technology has succeeded in producing virtually 'tamper proof' tagging (see Source I).

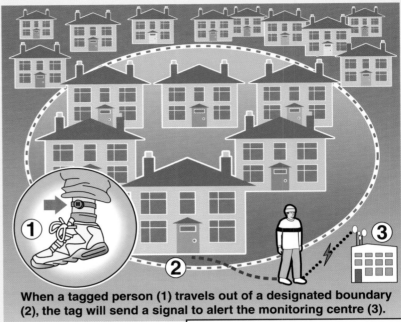

When a tagged person (1) travels out of a designated boundary (2), the tag will send a signal to alert the monitoring centre (3).

↑ **Source I**
Tagging – an alternative to prison?

Sending someone to prison for a year costs a minimum of £24 000. Tagging costs just £2 000 and could help to ease the strain on the prison system. Many believe that tagging should be used to keep track of past sex offenders. In stalking cases, an 'exclusion zone' can be created around the home of a victim. If the tagged offender gets too close, he or she triggers an alarm.

Some critics argue that it is a soft option. Others believe that it is too soon to say whether tagging helps to turn offenders away from crime. Is it desirable for society to have this sort of power over people?

Armed police

In recent years people have become more used to seeing armed police officers often at major airports. Almost every force now has armed response vehicles.

Despite these facts, the UK has a long tradition of unarmed police officers and the decision to introduce armed patrols on some inner-city housing estates has raised concerns. Opinion polls (see Source J) suggest that the majority do not want police carrying guns. Police officers themselves do not want to be armed. Some believe that if officers on the streets were armed more criminals would be encouraged to carry guns. They worry that it could be the first step on a slippery slope and that the risks should be kept in perspective.

Gun-related crime is still a very small element in our crime statistics. In 2000 there were about 4 000 armed incidents in England and Wales and 42 people died from gunshot wounds.

TASKS

1. In your opinion what are the best alternatives to prison?
2. 'Offenders should have the opportunity to make amends to society for their crimes.' Try to think of some of the ways they could do this.

Cybercrime

Cybercrime covers a huge range of illegal activity including financial scams, computer hacking, downloading certain images from the Internet, virus attacks, stalking by email and creating websites that promote racial hatred.

Computers have become a part of modern life and it is inevitable that some people see the 'wired world' as an opportunity to make money or cause trouble. The activities of some hackers can have disastrous results. For example, the 'love-bug' virus released on 4 May 2000 crippled at least 45 million computers worldwide and caused billions of pounds worth of damage. A 24-year-old Philippino student was arrested for programming the virus. The authorities had trouble deciding what laws applied in this case.

Some hackers break into the computer systems of banks and businesses, intent on stealing money or information like credit card numbers. Others trawl the Internet or other public databases for an individual's date of birth, social security number and address. This 'identity theft' is then used to apply for credit cards. Bogus companies are easily set up on the Internet. Unsuspecting buyers are offered low price products and are asked for their credit card details – then the site suddenly disappears. The dot com becomes a dot con!

The easy availability of pornography on the Internet, including material aimed at paedophiles, has helped to give the Internet a bad name. It is not just the police who are cracking down – many companies now routinely monitor the sites their employees visit online. Those who download offensive material run the risk of disciplinary action, or being fired.

Suggestions are frequently made to introduce laws to protect the law-abiding individual from cybercrime activities. Just like other initiatives we have looked at, concerns are expressed about possible infringements of the individual's privacy and liberty.

Few people dispute that a review of the criminal justice system is needed. The problem is how can it be done when opinions are so opposed?

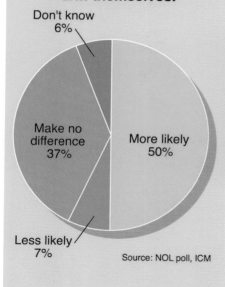

Police officers on routine street patrols should be armed.

Don't know 8%
Agree 34%
Disagree 58%

Source: NOL poll, ICM

Arming the police will make it more or less likely that criminals will also arm themselves.

Don't know 6%
Make no difference 37%
More likely 50%
Less likely 7%

Source: NOL poll, ICM

Source J ↑

TASK

'In the past, questions have been asked about how tough the justice system is but in recent years the questions have also centred on whether it is fair.'

Having read this section and undertaken some of the activities, do you think justice in the UK can be described as fair?

GCSE CHECK

| Importance of all members of society conforming to a common code of behaviour, including obedience of the law | Develop skills of searching for, selecting and effectively interpreting information | Knowledge of the role and operation of the criminal justice system |

A stable society

Aim

This section looks at society and by the end of the three case studies you will:

- understand some of the features of a pluralist democracy that help to create a stable society.

In the UK we live in a relatively stable society. We disagree about all sorts of things but we do so within the context of certain shared values. In unstable, divided societies there can be unrepresentative leaders, oppression, a lack of protection for weaker members of society, restrictions on freedom of speech and big social inequalities. In these case studies you will explore the UK's political and economic structures and what they mean to you as a citizen. It is because of structures like Parliament and concepts such as democracy and income tax that – in general – we live in a free, safe and relatively prosperous country.

Respect for old and established institutions?

The Queen is the head of state, but she follows the advice of the government of the day and cannot do what she wants. She officially appoints the Prime Minister after a General Election, declares Parliament open and closed, reads out the government policies at the start of every new Parliament and gives her approval or Royal Assent to any new laws. The Church of England is the established church in Britain – its leading representative, the Archbishop of Canterbury, often leads 'official' religious services.

Friendly relations with other countries?

The UK is one of the leading member states of the European Community. Close links are maintained with many other countries, notably within the Commonwealth, which links 50 independent nations, and the USA.

Respect for the authority, independence and fairness of the law courts and judges?

The law in the UK is upheld by a politically-accountable police force and an independent judicial system. Criminal law focuses on behaviour which the state has made illegal. Criminal offences are regarded as offences against the state; the Crown Prosecution Service therefore submits most criminal cases brought before the courts. Civil law concerns itself with the relationship between individuals, groups and organisations.

A commitment to improving public health and levels of education?

There has been a steady improvement in the general state of health of the British population, reflected by better nutrition, higher living standards, advances in medical science, better medical facilities and improved working conditions. The National Health Service (NHS) provides healthcare to all, regardless of income. There are widespread opportunities for people to learn, both at school and when older.

A shared set of values?

Nineteenth-Century political thinker John Stuart Mill stressed the importance of shared values in maintaining a stable society – and three in particular.

- Firstly, a system of education "which disciplines and restrains people from giving vent to their selfish and anti-social impulses".
- Secondly, a feeling of allegiance or loyalty to something – to a common God or gods, or to certain persons. "Something which is settled, something permanent, and not to be called in question; something which, by general agreement, has a right to be where it is ...".

- Finally, Mill felt it was important to have a feeling of common interest among those who lived in the same society. "A feeling of nationality may have been generated by ... the effect of identity of race and descent. Community of language, and community of religion, greatly contribute to it. Geographical limits are one of its causes. But the strongest of all is the possession of ... a national history ... collective pride and humiliation, pleasure and regret, connected with the same incidents in the past."

Long-standing political structures?

The UK's democratic system of parliamentary government is long established and has provided considerable political stability. There may not be a written constitution but basic freedoms and human rights are guaranteed by statute law.

Quality of life?

The UK is in the top ten out of 160 countries on a human development index that studies life expectancy, education levels and basic purchasing power to establish the quality of life of its citizens. More people than ever before own their homes and 75% of households have the use of a car. Consumer items are common and new technologies – such as DVDs – quickly become popular. Deprivation remains – primarily in inner cities – and the government spends £5 billion a year trying to improve conditions.

TASKS

1. What were the three types of shared values that Mill thought helped to make Britain a stable society in the Nineteenth Century?
2. Do you think that there are a set of shared values that help to bind British people together in the early Twenty-first Century?
3. Working in groups, rank in order of importance the eight answers suggested here as to why Britain is a relatively stable society. Justify your top three answers.
4. If you had the power to change one thing about British society to make it fairer, more democratic or more tolerant, what would you choose and why?

Freedom of the press and expression?

The UK possesses lively broadcast media, reflecting all shades of opinion. Abuses of power are unlikely to escape public exposure for long.

Why bother to vote?

Aim

You will:

- appreciate how you can make a difference by voting
- persuade other people that voting is important
- understand how the electoral system works in Britain
- explain some of the advantages and disadvantages of different voting systems.

Speech bubble 1: YOU SURRENDER YOUR RIGHT TO COMPLAIN IF YOU DONT TAKE PART- AT LEAST I'M HAVING A SAY.

Speech bubble 2: MEN AND WOMEN LIKE THE CHARTISTS AND THE SUFFRAGETTES BATTLED HARD FOR MY RIGHT TO VOTE. I'M NOT THROWING THAT AWAY LIGHTLY.

Speech bubble 3: THERE'S A LINK BETWEEN MY CROSS ON THE BALLOT PAPER, THE SIZE OF MY CHILD'S CLASS AND HOW LONG MY MUM HAS TO WAIT FOR AN NHS OPERATION.

POLLING STATION

↑ Source A

Citizenship and voting

Voting is central to democracy. For most people it is their only political act. Voting gives people a say in how things are to be done. Laws passed by governments determine the way in which a country, county, town, city, or village is run. So voting influences how the society in which we live is structured and organised. Society can be changed through political processes and actions. Political processes affect many aspects of our lives including what we learn at school, the price of goods in the shops, payment for medicines, how much tax we pay and many other things.

It is possible to make a real difference by voting. People can make sure that their opinion is shared with community leaders. Voting for local councillors or Members of Parliament (MPs or MEPs) who will take key decisions affecting us is not just a right, but also a duty of all adults. If you are a British citizen, when you turn 18 you will have the right to vote in local, national and European elections.

One of the main reasons that Citizenship has been introduced into schools is because of falling levels of political participation and interest, particularly amongst young people. Yet there are many places in the world where people do not have the right to vote. There is little to stop rulers and governments doing as they please. This leads to restrictions on people's rights and freedoms, as was seen in Nazi Germany.

TASKS

1. Why do you think that so many young people have little or no interest in politics?
2. What would make them more interested?

How could more people be persuaded to use their votes?

Increasing voter apathy was demonstrated in the 2001 UK General Election when only 59% of the electorate voted, the lowest turnout since 1918. Only about one-third of people now bother to vote at local council contests or elections to the European parliament. More people voted in Channel 4's *Big Brother* final than in the European elections in 2000!

Year	Electorate	Turnout *
1979	41 095 649	76.0
1983	42 192 999	72.7
1987	43 180 753	75.3
1992	43 249 721	77.7
1997	43 765 391	71.5
2001	44 405 826	59.4

*total valid vote as a % of the electorate

←Source B
Turnout at British elections 1979–2001.

Change Britain's 'first-past-the-post' electoral system to a more 'proportional' system, which gives each vote a greater weight in deciding the final outcome

Make tabloid newspapers give more space to political issues and debates and less space to celebrity news and scandal

Improve voter education amongst young people and the general public

Have Saturday or Sunday as the main day for voting (or poll over several days)

Make it easier for people to vote at different places (for example, supermarkets)

Make the politicians and political parties present themselves and their policies to the electorate with more conviction and credibility

Modernise the voting processes, for example by allowing people to vote by phone or on the Internet

Have a new section on the ballot paper to abstain or vote for 'none of the above'

Make it compulsory for people to vote (Australians are forced to register a vote by the threat of a fine)

TASKS

1. How might voter turnout be increased in British elections? Look at the nine statements. Working in pairs, set them in a diamond shape with what you think is the most important statement at the top, two equal statements on the next row, three equal statements on the next row, two on the next and the least important on the bottom. Can you agree on a diamond that represents the ideas of all the class? Your teacher might let you discard one statement and replace it with an idea of your own.
2. Look at Source A. Why have the people coming out of the polling station decided to vote?

Should voting be compulsory?

Source C
Should voting be compulsory?

FOR

✓ Helping to choose a government and to elect representatives is a civic duty as well as a right.

✓ Abstentions should be positively recorded on the ballot paper rather than expressed by non-attendance.

AGAINST

✗ There is something contradictory about making a 'free election' compulsory, or requiring people to exercise their rights.

✗ Low voter turnout is an important sign of faults in the democratic process.

In 1994, for the first time in its history, South Africa held democratic elections which included all of its citizens. Before this there had been a system of apartheid where the different colours and races, white, Indian and black, were treated differently. People walked and queued for hours in order to vote. The African National Congress (ANC), led by Nelson Mandela, won most seats and formed the government. Why do you think that the turnout was so high in this election?

→ **Source D**
Voting queue for the South African election.

Why do many young adults not vote?

Non-voting has many causes. Sometimes it is due to illness or to work obligations on polling day. For a few it may represent active hostility to the whole political process. Much more often it reflects ignorance or indifference – for example, not knowing about postal voting. In the 1992 and 1997 general elections, the numbers of people not voting was twice as high for those in traditional manual jobs as those in professional jobs. Turnout was also higher amongst:

• the elderly than the young
• the employed than the unemployed
• married as opposed to unmarried voters
• those who have lived longer in the same place
• settled communities and among the middle-aged and elderly.

Turnout is at its lowest among the young in deprived areas.

Votes at 16?

Various groups support the campaign to reduce the voting age from 18 to 16 including the British Youth Council, the Children's Rights Alliance, National Youth Agency, the Black Youth Forum and the youth sections of some of the political parties. The issue has been raised in Parliament and received some support from MPs of all the main parties. If you are interested in joining in, why not contact your local MP?

Source E

"We cannot attribute young people's lack of interest or participation in politics simply to a sense of disengagement from old-style politics ... The young have always been less interested in politics than their elders, partly no doubt because they have more pressing things on their minds – not only sex and music, but also finding jobs and homes. We also know that interest in politics does begin to assert itself more strongly as people become taxpayers and mortgage-holders ... with something to lose as well as something to gain.

It is likely that active citizenship is a habit that needs to be acquired early in life ... Eventually it does add up to a democratic deficit. If, for instance, you do not vote at your first and second opportunity to do so, and the world does not collapse as a result, well, why bother in the future?"

**R. Powell & A. Park, 'Young People, Politics and Citizenship: A Disengaged Generation?'
Citizenship Foundation Conference (1997)**

Old enough to pay taxes
but not to decide which politicians spend them

Old enough to get married and have kids
but not to vote on education policy

Old enough to die for your country
but not to elect the people who send you to war

IT'S TIME 16 YEAR OLDS WERE TREATED AS ADULTS Votes@16

TASKS

1. What is the evidence that young people are a 'disengaged generation'?
2. Read Source F. What are the arguments in favour of young people having the vote at 16? List the arguments that might be put forward against this idea.

←Source F
Poster produced by the Electoral Reform Society – one of the organisations in favour of votes at 16.

How the system works

There are a variety of ways in which votes can be turned into representation in an assembly or parliament. One way is for the candidate who gets the most votes in each constituency to be declared the winner and to represent that area in Parliament.

The current system for electing MPs to the House of Commons is called 'first-past-the-post'. There are 659 separate constituencies across the UK each electing an MP. In order to vote you simply put an 'X' next to the name of the candidate you support on your ballot paper. The candidate who gets the most votes wins, regardless of whether he or she has more than 50% support. Once members have been individually elected, the party with the most seats in Parliament, regardless of whether or not it has a majority of all votes cast across the country, normally becomes the next government. The system is used for national and local elections in the UK, Canada and India.

Arguments for the 'first-past-the-post' system of voting

- It is simple to understand.
- The voter can express a view on which party should form the next government.
- The system tends to produce single party governments, which are strong enough to create legislation and tackle the country's problems.
- It provides a close link between the MP and their constituency.
- The candidate with the greatest support wins through a fair process.
- Britain's democracy is one of the strongest in the world, it works and since no system is perfect, why should we go through the massive overhaul of changing it?
- Other electoral systems sometimes produce weak governments because there is often a need for coalitions (alliances with other parties).

Arguments against the 'first-past-the-post' system of voting

- Only one MP is elected in each constituency, so all the voters who did not vote for him or her are not represented. Their votes do not help elect anybody.
- In 1997 in Britain, 14.7 million voters cast ineffective votes – that is 48.2% of those who voted.
- There is a lack of choice given to the voters. The candidates are selected by a small number of party members.
- Voters are represented unequally. In 1997, the average number of votes per MP elected was: 32 376 for Labour, but 113 826 for Liberal Democrats.
- Parties focus entirely on winning the votes of a few hundred thousand 'swing' voters in marginal constituencies.
  - Parties are not currently choosing many female candidates or those from minority ethnic groups to fight 'winnable' seats.
  - Some people vote 'tactically' against the candidate they least favour rather than positively supporting the candidate closest to their views.

→**Source G**
Where are all the decisions made? The Houses of Parliament at Westminster.

A STABLE SOCIETY

Why bother to vote?

An ICM State of the Nation Poll for the Joseph Rowntree Reform Trust, in October 2000, measured reaction to the following statement:

"This country should adopt a new voting system that would give parties seats in Parliament in proportion to their share of votes."

	Total	England	London	Scotland	Wales
Strongly agree	31%	31%	27%	36%	28%
Tend to agree	29%	28%	24%	34%	27%
Neither agree nor disagree	14%	15%	10%	9%	13%
Tend to disagree	7%	7%	14%	5%	7%
Strongly disagree	8%	8%	21%	7%	9%
Don't know	11%	11%	4%	9%	16%

←Source H
Changing our electoral systems.

Some groups, such as the Electoral Reform Society and Charter 88, argue in favour of proportional representation. They aim to provide parties with a ratio of seats as close as possible to their share of the vote in elections. They also aim to ensure that minorities as well as majorities are represented. Part of the vote for the Scottish and Welsh Assembly is counted in this way.

There are many different versions of proportional representation and these systems have their critics too. Public opinion seems to be in favour of change. There may be a referendum on the question of electoral reform in the future. A referendum is when the electorate have a direct vote on a single issue.

TASKS

1. Draw three conclusions about public opinion and electoral reform from the information on these pages.
2. Why do you think that governments do not hold referendums more often?

You and voting

You may already have been involved with voting if your school has run a mock election. One of the best ways to learn about voting and electoral processes is to set up a class election.

TASKS

1. Organise an election for a class representative. Small groups can work together to decide on policies and aims. Choose a subject or policy issue. Choose one member of each group to be a candidate and prepare a short presentation to explain their policies to the rest of the class. Decide what voting system you are going to use, vote by secret ballot and have a returning officer announce the result.
2. You are going to create bookmarks to provide adults with basic information about local elections and motivate adults into voting.

You need to find out about the councillors who represent your area. To do this you might use email, letters, printed materials (flyers, brochures, pamphlets), field trips or guest speakers to gather information. You can also research relevant information about recent local elections and voting behaviour. Your bookmarks should encourage and provide reasons for voting and/or give some local election information. You might distribute the finished bookmarks through the local library, banks, garages or newsagents.

GCSE CHECK

Playing an active part in democratic and electoral processes

The media's role in society in providing information and affecting opinion

Developing skills of using statistics

Active participation in the school and wider community

Develop and apply knowledge about becoming informed citizens

Politicians –
what do they do
and how do they affect you?

Aim

You will:

- begin to understand the 'point' of politics, and why politics and politicians have a bad image
- gain an idea of how Parliament, MPs and political parties work
- understand the functions of local government
- consider some ways in which you might bring about political change.

↑ **Source A**
The Ancient Greeks invented politics and the concept of democracy. Before this there was 'oligarchy'. Find out what this means.

What is politics?

The Ancient Greeks invented 'politics' – the word comes from the word 'polis' meaning city. In around 400–500 BC some Greek cities such as Athens drew up laws to bring together the people of the city (citizens) in an assembly. Here, they discussed and argued issues that affected them all and tried to come to an agreement. This was the first working democracy. Democracy also comes from a Greek word – 'demokratia' – which means power by the people.

It was new for ordinary people to have a say in the decisions that affected their lives. Each Athenian citizen had an equal right to take part in discussions and votes on laws and policies. In some ways this is more democratic than the systems we know today because citizens took part in person ('direct democracy'). Today's 'representative democracies' are indirect and citizens are at least one step removed from the decision-making processes of government. However, Athenian democracy was not all perfect! Citizenship was restricted to freeborn males – it excluded women, slaves and resident foreigners. Similar restrictions existed in most Western systems until well into the Twentieth Century. For example, British women could not vote in elections until 1918, and only about 60% of men were eligible to vote before this date.

Society has to be organised if the people living in it are to work and live together happily. In developed, democratic countries laws prevent people harming others and protect the weak. There are structures in place to provide hospitals for the sick and schools for children. There are roads for transport, and people have sufficient money to buy food. People also need a roof over their heads and a clear understanding of what their civil rights and responsibilities are. Politics is about discussing and debating how a society is organised, governed and changed and then getting things done.

The job of politicians is to represent their constituents – the people from the area that elected them. They also represent their parties' interests and try to keep promises made in their manifestos (a manifesto is a public statement outlining a political plan of action). Politicians have the power to make laws, raise taxes and decide how public money is allocated and spent.

The image of politics and politicians

Many people say that they dislike politics and politicians. They don't trust them. Citizens all over the world dislike political activity that produces few results and politicians that do not seem to speak their language or listen to them. Why?

- Some politicians may appear to be more interested in personal power and ambition than representing the electorate.
- Because the House of Commons is televised, the public sees fairly juvenile behaviour from MPs at Prime Minister's Question Time, and an empty room on many other occasions.
- The stereotypical image is overwhelmingly of middle-aged and middle class men in suits. Women, minority ethnic groups and young people are under-represented amongst MPs.
- Politicians rarely seem to give a direct answer when interviewed. They often appear to spend their time criticising opponents. They rarely seem to 'own up' when things go wrong.

Source B

"The challenge for politicians is to show people that politics can be a good path for people's criticisms. So, I want to see politicians and politics become more responsive to the needs and views of the public. That is an important part of building a reputation, not just for individual parties but for the whole of politics. I want to see politicians become more reliable, and to be seen to be more reliable. And I want to see politicians become more reputable, which is after all what this is all about. Only if politicians connect with voters, and are seen to care about the issues which matter to the whole of the population, can we hope to improve our reputation, and win the battle against apathy. The battle for reputation should ... help us find a way of connecting politicians and voters, through combining image, message and reality. ... By descending into the realms of cheap jokes and personal insults, the reputation of politicians is plummeting. We don't only need to persuade the public that our particular party has the best policies, we need to persuade them that politicians are worth voting for at all. ..."

Speech by Charles Kennedy, Leader of the Liberal Democrat Party (12 November 2001)

←Source C
Prime Minister's Question Time takes place every Wednesday when Parliament is in session.

TASKS

1. In pairs brainstorm words and phrases that come into your head when you think how politics and politicians are reported in the media.
2. Read Source B. Why does Charles Kennedy think that people have lost faith in politicians?

How does the British political system work?

Parliament

Parliament is made up of the House of Commons and the House of Lords, with the Queen playing a figurehead role. Parliament's main responsibilities are:

- to make laws
- to keep an eye on the government's spending
- to monitor how the government runs the country
- to debate the big issues of the day.

Some of the law-making powers have been given to the National Assembly for Wales, the Scottish Parliament and the Northern Ireland Assembly (see Case Studies 1 and 3). In the future there may be regional English parliaments – for example, for the South-West or North of England.

Parliament keeps a check on the government in other ways. These include:

- Parliamentary select committees which question ministers and civil servants about their work.
- Question Time, a period set aside each day when MPs can put questions to ministers.

A Parliament cannot last longer than five years and is divided up into sessions that usually last a year. Note that Parliament is not the same thing as the government, even though the government is largely made up of elected Members of Parliament (MPs).

Government

Most MPs belong to a particular political party. The main three British parties are the Labour Party, the Conservative Party and the Liberal Democrat Party. The party which has the most MPs elected across the United Kingdom constituencies in a general election then forms the government. The leader of the most popular party becomes Prime Minister. S/he then appoints a cabinet of around 20 leading ministers. There is no official list of rules saying exactly what the government's powers are or what treatment ordinary people should expect from it. The judiciary – or legal system – puts laws into practice.

> **↓ Source D**
> Membership of the House of Lords is undergoing reform. It includes a mixture of bishops, judges and life peers – who are people appointed for their expertise and experience in various aspects of public life such as politics, education, medicine or business. Because members are not elected, some people think they are out of touch.

An MP's week

Lembit Opik is the Liberal Democrat MP for Montgomeryshire in Wales. He is the party's spokesman on Northern Ireland, Young People and Welsh Affairs.

Monday

My 105-hour-long working week starts on Monday morning, generally in my constituency. I go down to my office and do paperwork and look at the week ahead. Then after spending up to lunchtime at meetings – local farmers' markets, say – I'll come down to London. Usually I cheat on Mondays and look at all the interesting stuff. In the evening, I'll attend internal party meetings.

Tuesday

I come into the office and look over my paperwork until my first meeting, which could be anything from the British Gliding Association to the National Farmers Union. And then there's meeting after meeting, and interviews, and occasionally going to the House [of Commons] to make a contribution to a statement. There's a mixture of briefings and lunches and dinners where you're expanding your circle of influence. Sometimes I'm naughty and let myself have just a social evening. And then there's usually a vote at ten in the House of Commons.

Wednesday

Wednesday is a big day. Prime Minister's Question Time gives it a big impetus. Consequently, its the longest day in terms of work - once again, the usual mix of paperwork and meetings. There's also the parliamentary party's meeting where we discuss where the party's going and perhaps have a few discussions on strategy. I usually visit Stranger's Bar, which is an oasis of political interaction. That's a place where a lot of business gets done.

Thursday

On Thursdays, things get quieter again. Maybe there's a debate in the House or something that you have to attend. But there tends to be a lot of paperwork. And then Thursday evening, it's back to the constituency.

Friday

Friday, it's constituency work. I do things like going to visit the local rubbish tip to talk about the environment, opening a playground, giving a talk to a local school, meeting local business people, showing a visiting minister around, that kind of thing.

Saturday

Saturday tends to be surgery day. And then, occasionally, there's a bit of shopping. Saturday night is the night that I usually go out in the constituency. Unless I'm doing an after-dinner speech.

Sunday

And Sunday's the day that I pretend that I'm going to have off. I end up having meetings but I don't call them meetings so that I can pretend that I'm not working.

What can one MP do for a cause?

Having an MP or member of the House of Lords on your side has lots of advantages. They can:

- Ask questions in Parliament to various ministers. As this is covered on TV and in the newspapers, this could get the story in the papers.
- Request private meetings with the relevant minister.
- Speak publicly about the issue.
- Propose a private member's bill that suggests a new law on the subject.

TASKS

1. Look at Source D. What sort of people do you think should be members of the House of Lords and why?
2. What skills help people to be effective and politically active? Read 'An MP's week' and then write a 150-word job description outlining the various qualities an MP should have.

What does local government do?

All parts of Britain are divided into administrative regions called councils or unitary authorities. Elected councils exist at the level of city, county, town or village. This is called local government. Local government has responsibility for areas such as:

- protective services, for example fire, police, consumer protection, lighting, security cameras in public places
- environmental services, for example roads, transport, refuse collection and recycling
- personal services, for example schools, social services (such as children's homes or the 'Meals on wheels' service for the elderly)
- recreational services, for example parks, sports centres and libraries
- commerce, for example markets, restaurants, transport
- promotion of the area, for example employment creation, tourism, economic regeneration
- regulations, for example implementing national and European laws and monitoring standards.

Councils set levels of local taxation to pay for locally-run services. Local politics is the process of settling differences and reaching compromises over local issues. It involves local elections, parties, pressure groups, media and local opinion. Local government exists in virtually all developed countries and is generally seen as a sign of a healthy democracy – a check on central government power.

Nevertheless, many powers were taken away from local government in the 1980s and have not been restored. Perhaps connected with this, decreasing numbers of people are interested in local government and politics. Some European countries give more powers to their equivalent of British county councils, metropolitan authorities and town councils.

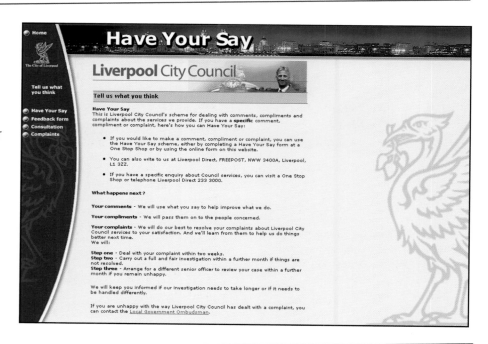

↑ **Source E**
Part of the Liverpool City Council website, encouraging citizens to engage with the Council to improve its services.

Increasing participation beyond the ballot box?

These are some suggestions for increasing popular interest in local government issues:

- Citizens' juries – bringing together groups of 12–16 representative members of the community to consider an issue in depth.
- Standing citizens' panels comprising a sample, statistically representative of the population, to act as sounding boards.
- Area-based neighbourhood committees.
- Tenants' and residents' groups.
- Interest- and user-group forums (perhaps including youth councils).
- Local referendums.
- Public question times at council meetings.
- Interactive technology using the Internet to inform and find out people's views.

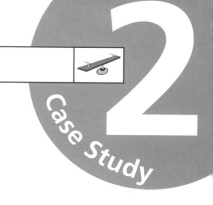

You and politics

It is easy to see government as something 'done by other people', 'out there', and something that does not affect you. In fact there is plenty of scope for you to make a difference. Politicians hold office because of people like you. You have the right to demand their help. You might contact an MP or councillor:

- If you have a problem that is difficult to solve and you need help in arguing your case. For example, someone who feels badly treated by their local hospital might ask for help from their MP. Someone worried about the speed of traffic outside a school might contact a councillor.

- If you want to lobby or pressurise the council or government into taking action on a specific issue. For example, you could ask your MP to press the government to bring in legislation to ban the live export of animals. Your MP could then ask the Secretary of State for the Environment and Rural Affairs about the issue in the House of Commons.

- Through writing a letter. This gives them time for reflection and research and it is more convenient for busy politicians to read your letters than to see you. Outline the issue that concerns you, summarise your position, ask a couple of questions and then note the reasons why your MP or councillor should adopt the policies you recommend. You should get a response, but don't expect them automatically to agree with you!

Source F

"We aim at no less than a change in the political culture of this country both nationally and locally: for people to think of themselves as active citizens, willing, able and equipped to have an influence in public life and with the critical capabilities to weigh evidence before speaking and acting."

From the final report of the Advisory Group on Citizenship, chaired by Professor Sir Bernard Crick (1998)

What is democracy?

The success of youth and school councils has made young people realise that it is important to have an official voice where decisions are being made – in Parliament. The first elections for the UK Youth Parliament (UKYP) took place at the end of 2000. Any young person, resident in the UK and aged 11–18 can vote and stand for election, provided they attend their local Election Day. Every Local Education Authority (LEA) across the country was asked to host an election for the UKYP. At least one MYP (Member of the Youth Parliament) was chosen by each LEA.

Those elected will be able to talk to MPs about the issues that affect young people everywhere – from curfews and fair wages to the number of teenage pregnancies. They will also create a Youth Manifesto, which will be presented to the three main political parties and service providers for young people for them to respond to.

TASKS

1. Look at the functions of local government. Councillors like to consult the electorate and hear its views on particular issues. Several, like Sheffield, have websites so that you can communicate your views. Choose one council service, or a current 'hot' issue from your area. 'Say your piece' to the council about a particular problem with the service in your locality and what you would like done about it. Give reasons and examples to back up your opinions.

2. i) What do you think might be achieved by a Youth Parliament in Britain?
   ii) What difficulties might a Youth Parliament face?

Tackling political and social problems

Some problems do not have easy political solutions and there is not just one straightforward answer. Soon after being elected in 1997, the Labour government created a Social Exclusion Unit to analyse problems in the 1300 most deprived neighbourhoods of Britain. Its first report attacked the way that central and local government had failed these neighbourhoods in the past. Not enough emphasis had been placed on the communities themselves. It also claimed that previous funds had been wasted because of a lack of co-ordination.

The feedback from 18 policy action teams working in deprived communities formed the basis for a national strategy for neighbourhood renewal launched in January 2001. Read the account of one such community (see Source H) and then consider some of the options available to improve the life of residents.

Source G

"These are handsome, postwar, semi-detached houses with gardens …[but]… few people want to live here at any price. Brian Mumby, chairman of the Halton Moor Estate Management Board tells a familiar story. 'When I moved to this estate it was Utopia. The kids even obeyed the 'Keep off the Grass' signs.' Brian has travelled the world and 'seen real poverty, people without food, without water, without clothes'. …'These people are not poor,' he says.

He goes on to talk about the dependency culture and the apathy of his fellow tenants. … We are talking in the upstairs committee room of the [newly built] Halton Moor One Stop and Community Centre. At the One Stop you can pay your rent, enquire about your benefits, visit your probation officer, talk to your social worker, and every week for three-quarters of an hour you can consult your local councillor. The Community Centre is one room shared by a pensioners' group, mothers and toddlers, and the Youth Forum. The main activity of the Youth Forum is running bingo sessions for the pensioners. The two youth workers based here are responsible for the whole of east Leeds.

Brian confirms that most of the problems on the estate are caused by youths, then tells me the youth club is only open two hours a week. He is aware of the irony. Halton Moor was given £23 million by a Conservative government under the Urban Renewal Funding Scheme in 1992. It has been spent on renovations, fortifications and anti-joyriding measures. The money will be gone and the work completed by spring 2002, yet the renovations are now being renovated. Boy racers have turned joyriding into a synchronised sport. … Mostly the police don't attend, and the boys and the stolen cars converge on the large green at Ullswater Crescent. The green has been extensively landscaped … to prevent such a happening, but these boy racers rise to the challenge and make the cars leap the obstacles. After grass-churning victory circuits they jump from the cars and set fire to them. It is certainly more exciting than handing out bingo cards to pensioners.

There is a row of village-style shops overlooking the green. Only one, the newsagent's, is open. Brian wants to demolish this eyesore and build a community centre here. Leeds City Council has offered him £150 000. He needs a million-and-a-half and plans to go to the EU and the Lottery for the money. …

In the car park afterwards we watch families arriving and departing in expensive cars. They are going into the other entrance – to the East Leeds Leisure Centre whose facilities include a sports hall, sun beds, creche and swimming pool. Brian tells me the families are from outside and '… the local people can't afford to use it'. Brian has negotiated a deal whereby local children can swim for 30p a session in the summer holidays. The only time the pool is full.

The next day there are three burnt-out cars on Ullswater Green. Malcolm rides up on his bike. He looks into the gaping bonnets of the cars with almost professional interest. … I ask why joyriding is so popular here. 'It's a crap estate.' I ask if things have improved since a Labour government was elected. 'No, if owt, it's got crapper. …'

It suits the main political parties to talk about voter apathy. They like to give the impression that the electorate is too idle to tear itself away from its sofa and TV screens to walk to the local scout hut to make its mark. The Halton Moor estate electorate is as lively and intelligent as any group of people I've met. They are largely contemptuous of politicians and their passionless double-speak. The withdrawal of their vote shows their contempt. The very poor are getting poorer, and nobody seems to care."

Sue Townsend writing in *The Observer* (20 May 2001)

TASKS

1. Read Source G. Working in pairs, note some questions that you would like to ask national and local politicians about the problems on this estate.
2. You have been appointed to a policy action team responsible for neighbourhood renewal. Which of the solutions on housing, crime, community and political attention would you adopt and why? Which would you reject? Can you think of some other solutions?
3. Why should society and politicians 'care' about estates like Halton Moor?

Politicians – what do they do and how do they affect you?

Housing and the environment

- Re-house trouble-makers away from problem estates.
- Knock down uninhabitable houses.
- Immediately repair or improve houses which are in danger of becoming derelict.
- Encourage local businesses to contribute to improvement projects through a voluntary business rate or offering them financial incentives.

Crime

- Appoint neighbourhood wardens to back up the police and try to combat nuisance behaviour.
- Increase punishments for criminal behaviour.
- Bring in 'curfews' to keep convicted trouble-makers in at night.
- Increase police presence in the area.
- Increase anti-crime activities in local schools.

Increase the sense of community

- Increase funding for a community centre (but the council has a limited budget).
- Give financial incentives to shop owners to move back into the area.
- Set targets to reduce the time it takes to remove abandoned cars.
- Encourage community projects in local schools.
- Consult closely with local people and give a stronger voice to people within local communities.

Give more political attention to the problems

- Tackle the poverty and unemployment that lies at the roots of many of the problems.
- 'Name and shame' the problem estates in the media.
- Establish a long-term plan to close the gap between the richest and poorest areas of the country.
- Help residents and councillors bid for improvement funds from the European Union or National Lottery.
- Raise income tax or local council taxes to invest in some of the more deprived housing estates.

GCSE CHECK

The work of parliament and government in making and shaping laws	The importance of playing an active part in democratic processes	The opportunity for individuals to bring about change locally and nationally	Research a topical political/social issue by analysing information from different sources	Negotiate and take part responsibly in school-based group activities

How does the **global economy** work?

Aim

You will:

- begin to understand some of the basic ways in which the local, national and world economies work and how we influence them as consumers and workers.

Like money?

Use a coin as your counter and throw a dice to play the game.

Instructions

Play the game to the end. Roll the dice and every time you land on a circle, copy the text into your book as bullet points. By the end of the game you should have a record or list of your moves. Does it look like a bright financial future? What knowledge and skills will you need to ensure your life is a financial success?

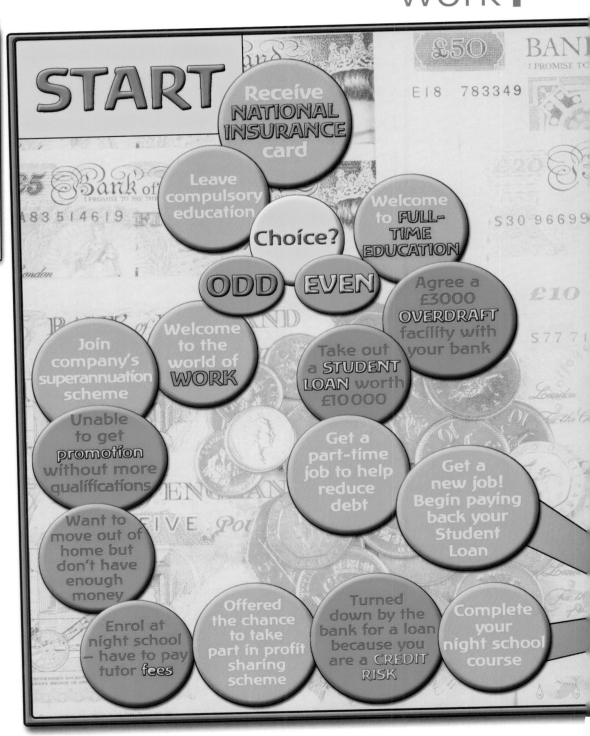

START

- Receive NATIONAL INSURANCE card
- Leave compulsory education
- Choice?
- Welcome to FULL-TIME EDUCATION
- ODD
- EVEN
- Agree a £3000 OVERDRAFT facility with your bank
- Join company's superannuation scheme
- Welcome to the world of WORK
- Take out a STUDENT LOAN worth £10 000
- Unable to get promotion without more qualifications
- Get a part-time job to help reduce debt
- Get a new job! Begin paying back your Student Loan
- Want to move out of home but don't have enough money
- Enrol at night school – have to pay tutor fees
- Offered the chance to take part in profit sharing scheme
- Turned down by the bank for a loan because you are a CREDIT RISK
- Complete your night school course

How does something get a price?

The price of any item is only set by what the consumer is prepared to pay for it. Manufacturers and retailers estimate the prices they think people will pay for goods, and we think no more of it. But how prices can change is in the main influenced by the principles of supply and demand.

Consider the example of the mobile phone. Over the last five years there has been a huge increase in the UK in the number of people owning mobile telephones. Many of you will probably have one of your own, but as little as ten years ago very few people had one. Why is this? Was there no demand for them? There was demand but only at a very low level and from a specific sort of customer. The main explanation of the explosion in mobile phone ownership is the price. In 1985 the price of the technology to make a mobile phone was very expensive, as was the creation of transmitter masts and satellites. With a mobile phone costing approximately £2000, few people could afford to use one.

2002

Today phone technology is cheaper. Manufacturers and telecommunications companies invested heavily to bring phone prices down. Demand is now being met by supply so most of the population now own one. The price is determined by a relationship between what we, the consumer, can afford and how much it costs a company to make.

1985

Items like mobile phones are called goods but the same pricing principles apply to services, such as a bus service or using a leisure centre.

TASKS

Think about the manufacturer of a pair of trainers and answer the following.

a) What sort of materials are used to make a pair of trainers? How much do they cost and where do they come from?

b) What will it cost to make the finished pair of trainers? Think about the sort of processes

needed to make the trainers, and the different people involved.

c) What will it cost to transport and then sell them?

d) Now think about how much you would be willing to pay for a pair of trainers. Are they a designer label? Are certain brands priced higher than others? Why do you think this is?

What influences decisions on taxation and spending in the UK?

What is taxation?

Taxation – or tax – is money 'levied' or taken by the government from people and businesses to pay for services, such as hospitals, roads, defence or the emergency services.

Who decides how much tax will be levied?

The government, but especially the Chancellor of the Exchequer, decides on how much tax we pay. Every year the Chancellor decides on how much money will be taken in tax and matches this with the amount of money the government is proposing to spend (expenditure) (see Source B).

How are these decisions made?

There are no right or wrong ways for governments to balance spending and taxation. Many individuals and businesses would like to pay less tax, even though we are one of the lowest taxed countries in Europe already. But paying less tax inevitably means there is less income for the government to allocate to public services, which are in desperate need of major investment. Source A shows some of the pressures on taxation levels.

Source A

Taxation pressures

- Business organisations like the Confederation of British Industry (CBI) and the Chambers of Commerce want lower business taxes.
- Sometimes taxes have to be raised because the economy is 'over-heating'; for example, house prices are rising too rapidly.
- Political promises are made not to raise taxes to help get a political party elected, or to keep taxes low because the party is unpopular.
- Increase 'indirect' tax, for example Value Added Tax

(VAT). But this is often seen as unfair because goods or services cost the same to everyone, no matter how much they earn.
- Pressure from Trade Unions and low pay pressure groups to reduce tax burden on low paid workers.
- Money needed for government priority areas, for example health, education, and transport.
- Raising income tax could mean people will have less money to spend and so the economy could suffer.

Source B

Government spending in 1835 (right) and 2001 (below).

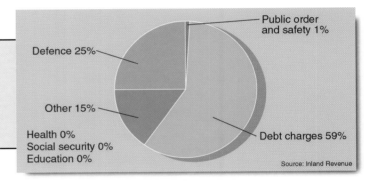

Defence 25%
Public order and safety 1%
Other 15%
Health 0%
Social security 0%
Education 0%
Debt charges 59%

Source: Inland Revenue

Department	£ billions	As a % of total spending
Social security	£123	31
NHS	£60	15
Transport	£11	3
Education	£50	13
Defence	£24	6
Debt interest	£22	5
Industry, agriculture and employment	£22	5
Housing and the environment	£19	5
Law and order	£23	6
Other expenditure	£44	11
Total	£398	

TASKS

1. Using the data from Source B, create your own pie charts for 2001 income and expenditure.
2. Describe the major changes in government expenditure from 1835–2001. What surprises you most about the changes?

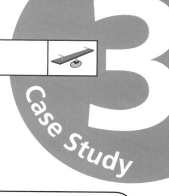

What I would do!

I'm a right-winger

I believe tax and spending should be decided as follows:

- Tax people less. If they earned the money they deserve it and will help make even more money for the economy, so creating more jobs.
- Government spending should focus more on defence and law and order. This type of spending creates a secure environment in which businesses can prosper.
- Spend less on social security. If there is no unemployment benefit then people will find work and so create wealth rather than take it.
- Encourage private companies to run public services. They will use their money to run hospitals and repair roads so we can tax people less. It's only right that they make a profit from this, and the more they do, the more willing they will be to take over service provision.

I'm a left-winger

I believe tax and spending should be decided as follows:

- Tax people more. You only need so much money. The richest people in the country are getting richer while the poor get poorer. Share the wealth.
- Increase tax on the very richest people and use it to provide public services for those who cannot afford them.
- Use the money raised by increased taxes to improve hospital care, train more doctors and nurses. Healthy workers can contribute more to the economy.
- Spend less on defence. The 'Cold War' is over, we don't need massive, very expensive armies.
- Spend more on education. The young people of our country are tomorrow's employees.

How else can we raise money for local and national government spending?

- Local councils can borrow more money to spend on better local services but they will have to pay interest on the loan.
- 'Contract out' services to the private sector. Your local sports centre may be owned by the local council but run by a private company who provides a service for profit, perhaps at a cheaper price than if it was operated by the council.
- Public/private sector agreements. This allows the government to create partnerships with private companies, who provide the money for schemes such as a transport network, in exchange for a share in the profits.

TASKS

1. Using the information on these pages, discuss in small groups what you would change about the amount of money spent in each government department as shown in Source B.
2. Your group has been given the job of drafting next year's government taxation and spending plans. Think carefully about how you feel about the arguments outlined above.
   - Would your total tax bill be more or less than 2001's £398 billion?
   - Would you raise more money to spend through tax or other means, like the changes to National Insurance in the 2002 budget?
   - What would you change about government expenditure and how could you justify your decisions?

   Write your answers up in a report and show the balance sheet for your budget.

An economic picture of Britain

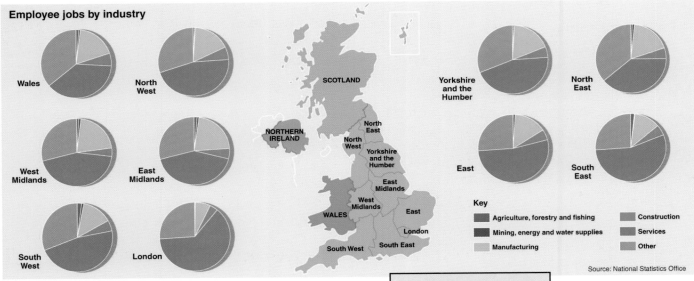

Employee jobs by industry

Wales

North West

West Midlands

East Midlands

South West

London

SCOTLAND

NORTHERN IRELAND

North East

North West

Yorkshire and the Humber

East Midlands

West Midlands

WALES

East

London

South West

South East

Yorkshire and the Humber

North East

East

South East

Key

- Agriculture, forestry and fishing
- Mining, energy and water supplies
- Manufacturing
- Construction
- Services
- Other

Source: National Statistics Office

↑ Source C
Employee jobs by industry.

In recent decades there have been many changes to the types of work people do. Source C shows this for the regions of England and Wales in 2001. The majority of workers are employed in the service sector but the sector for information technology, research and development, health, education and recreational/culture activities is now a very large employer. There are some regions, however, which still have a large dependency on manufacturing industries. These industries – and so the regions – have suffered as a result of cheaper goods being imported from abroad.

Source D shows the areas which receive economic help from the government. Generally these are areas of traditional heavy manufacturing employment.

Areas receiving economic help during the early 1990s

↑ Source D
Areas – marked in dark green – in England, Wales and Scotland receiving economic help during the 1990s.

TASKS

Write a letter to the Minister for Regional Development describing the economic situation in your region. Consider the following points.

- Is your area suffering from economic decline?
- Do you think it should receive government help? If so, what for and what sort of aid would be helpful?
- If your area has a larger share of new industries do you think other areas should receive more money?

Public/private sector

Look around you in the classroom. What things have been provided by the public and private sector? For example:

- your shoes
- whiteboard
- teacher
- books
- your shirt
- computers
- tables and chairs
- your pen
- carpet

What's the difference between the public and private sectors?

The private sector makes things or provides services for money and profit. The public sector provides goods and mainly services where profits can't be found. For example, it would be very difficult to get everyone on a street to chip-in to have the road repaired, but through local government taxes and spending this is done. However, public sector services can only be provided for the common good if money can be raised from taxes. This means we need wealth creation to take place and keep taking place, if we are to provide our communities with their needs.

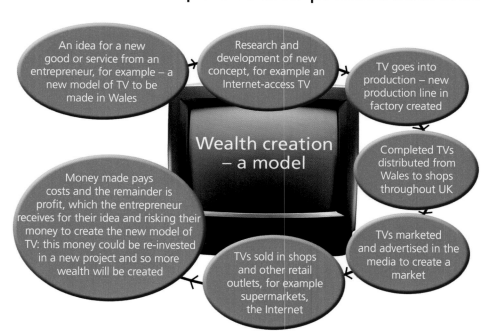

An idea for a new good or service from an entrepreneur, for example – a new model of TV to be made in Wales

Research and development of new concept, for example an Internet-access TV

TV goes into production – new production line in factory created

Wealth creation – a model

Completed TVs distributed from Wales to shops throughout UK

Money made pays costs and the remainder is profit, which the entrepreneur receives for their idea and risking their money to create the new model of TV: this money could be re-invested in a new project and so more wealth will be created

TVs marketed and advertised in the media to create a market

TVs sold in shops and other retail outlets, for example supermarkets, the Internet

TASKS

1. Think about the wealth creation model above – what costs will this manufacturing company have? How many different people will receive some sort of payment for their part in this process? Could you use this list to describe to someone else how the private sector creates wealth?

2. As a group discuss what services and goods you think should be provided by the public sector. Remember to justify your decisions.

3. Write up your answers in the form of a speech and use it to create a class debate on the future of the public sector.

Aspects of the global economy

Is trade between all countries of the world fair? Do some countries get a better deal than others?

The world of global trade

Local businesses export their goods overseas.

How are these organisations linked with the wider world?

Do they have to import raw materials? Do they have good transport links to help import and export goods – for example, roads, railways and ports?

How do they ensure safe and fair working conditions?

Are workers' rights/legislation national or universal?

What are the loan conditions?

To what extent is global trade 'fair'?

How can businesses influence the working conditions of those they trade with in other countries?

How could it be made fairer?

Solutions?

Trade agreements

Some international rules have been created to deal with trade between nations. The World Trade Organisation is the main example of this. At its heart are the WTO agreements, negotiated and signed by the bulk of the world's trading nations and ratified by their governments. The goal is to help producers of goods and services, exporters and importers to conduct their business.

Trade zones

Because of problems with import taxes levied by certain governments, some nations have joined together to form trade zones. Examples include the European Union, Latin Integration Association and the Organisation for Petroleum Exporting Countries. However, these groups often only look after the interests of their own members and even complicate the rules of trade.

> **Source E**
>
> "Everyone has the right to understand fully the nature of the 'economic' systems of which they are part, as a producer, as a consumer, as one among the billions of people populating the earth. They have the right to know the benefits from the fruits of their work, who benefits from what he buys and sells and the degree to which they enhance or degrade their planetary inheritance."
>
> **United Nations Meeting, Mexico (1974)**

Ethical business

For many people in the rich 'west' of the world, mass consumerism is a way of life. Many of us have little idea of how or where the goods we buy are made. If you look at the "Made in …" labels in your trainers, how many are made in this country with our employment and health and safety laws applying? Did anyone receive a fair wage for producing your footwear?

Anti-capitalist and green protests

Some people choose to protest against what they see as the rich gaining at the expense of the poor, and the destruction of the world's resources. They protest at any meetings where decisions about how world trade and therefore how millions of lives will be lived, are being made by the richest nations on the planet. Are they attempting to make things better for those who live in third world countries?

Fair trade

Our role in the global economy – how can we make a difference?

Every time we buy a good or service, someone either benefits in the form of employment or profit or is exploited. It is important that everyone benefits in a global economy and so some people buy from sources that help everyone in the production of goods get a fair deal.

"Fair trade is a good thing for farmers like me; we earn more, but it also means we get help and advice with farming practices and learn new skills, becoming better farmers. Being a member of Kuapa Kokoo has made me a better farmer."

Source F

"International trade may seem a remote issue, but when commodity prices fall dramatically it has a catastrophic impact on the lives of millions of small scale producers, forcing many into crippling debt and countless others lose their land and their homes.

The Fairtrade Foundation exists to ensure a better deal for marginalised and disadvantaged third world producers. The Foundation awards a consumer label, Fairtrade Mark, to products which meet internationally recognised standards of fair trade."

Guarantees **a better deal** for Third World Producers

The Fairtrade Foundation

Source G

"Life is hard for cocoa farmers – they are some of the poorest people in the world and on average earn about £50 a year. In Ghana, West Africa, there are about 2 million cocoa farmers. They depend on selling their beans to pay for the essential things in life, like school fees, doctors' bills, farm tools or wellington boots to protect their feet from the scorpions that live among the cocoa trees.

However, world prices for cocoa are now so low many farmers often can't even afford the basics, leaving them with no food, medicine, clean water or to pay for their children to go to school."

Comic Relief, Dubble Chocolate

TASKS

1. In what way do you, as a consumer and a future worker, affect the world economy?
2. What can you do to ensure that, as a citizen of the world, people from other countries are not exploited when you purchase goods and services?

GCSE CHECK

Understand how the economy works at local, national and international level	Appreciate your responsibilities and rights as a consumer, future employee and potential employer	Know that the government is responsible for managing the economy	Recognise the complexity of issues and make judgements supported by evidence	Understand 'fairness', 'financial capability' and 'education for sustainable development'

Making a change

Aim

This section looks at 'Making a change' and by the end of the three case studies you will:

- know what an individual or a group can do to improve their local area or the way in which they are treated
- understand how different organisations campaign for change
- know how people co-operate on a national or global level, in order to achieve change.

Introduction

"You make it light on yourself and let me have those seats."

These words seem unimportant but they helped to start a campaign that had major consequences. In 1950s America, black Americans faced discrimination. For those who lived in the southern states of the country all public facilities were segregated, such as swimming pools, cinemas and even cafés. Then one day, a middle-aged black American lady said 'No'. She refused to give up her seat on a bus to a white passenger and was arrested. Her name was Rosa Parks.

Her case made other black Americans in Montgomery, Alabama, take action. For over a year, black Americans in Montgomery boycotted the buses. They walked to work and school; they organised car pools for longer journeys and they attracted media interest in this example of a community working together. Using economic and moral pressure they eventually made the Supreme Court take action against segregation on buses. Other black Americans watched this story unfold in the media and they too took action. Some worked to desegregate cafés or bus stations, others worked to get changes in the laws. They were part of a civil rights movement which showed how individuals could join with others to take a stand against injustice.

Each year, many people make New Year resolutions on how they are going to improve their life: lose weight, join a gym, ditch the old boy/girlfriend and find their perfect match! In this way, people are trying to change their lives by identifying the areas they think need improvement. However, many people resolve not just to change their lives but work to change things for the better in the world around them. This section will look at how individuals and organisations can change things, in their local area, in their country and also globally.

←**Source A**
Rosa Parks being fingerprinted following arrest (1956).

GCSE CHECK

| Topical political, social and cultural issues and events | Identify how individuals and groups can play an active part in the process of change | Reflect on participation in movements for change | Express your views on issues and identify and explain the views of others |

In the case of the Montgomery Bus Boycott, the local black community had a clear example of one thing that needed improvement; who could change the law and how they could influence those people or institutions. Rosa Parks clearly understood the consequences of her refusal to move seats and she, and others, worked quickly to create support. In order to make change happen, individuals and groups need to identify the answers to the following questions.

How can we achieve change?

Problem and aims
What needs changing/what precise change do we want to happen?

Target for the campaign
Who or what can make this change happen?

Tactics
How can we influence them to make the changes that we want?

Anticipated consequences
What might be the consequences of our tactics? When do we need to review how far we have got in achieving our aims, and alter our plan of action, if necessary?

TASK

Read through the following situation and construct a diagram, similar to the one above which identifies the problem, the aims, the tactics and the possible methods of achieving change.

The local council has closed a small park due to vandalism and the park being used to sell and use drugs. The park is surrounded by iron railings in the centre of a built-up area. It is largely overgrown with several 'hidden' areas of shrubs and bushes. However, many parents want somewhere for young children to play. Local residents are also unhappy that the park is beginning to be used as an illegal tip and that the iron railings are also being stolen. The local residents group has decided that something needs to be done. What would be your advice?

Local issues –
can **young people** make a **difference**?

Aim

You will:

- understand how citizens can make a difference
- observe some ways individuals try to bring about change in national and local affairs
- add to your knowledge and understanding of democratic processes and ways in which individuals can take active roles in their local community.

↓ **Source A**
Housing being built on green belt land.

Stop the builders!

'Stop the builders!' and 'The builders are coming!' could be the headlines in almost any local newspaper in areas where there is pressure to find new land for housing developments. In this example, newspaper articles announced that the local council was in the process of proposing plans for 500 new houses to be built on what was believed to be green belt land. The council proposal even included changes to the designated green belt boundaries to allow the building to go ahead.

To prove its point, and generate dismay at the proposal, the local newspaper gave the following quote from a council planning committee document.

C1.19 The JSRP through policies 2(1), 9 and 16 states that a *change to the Green Belt boundary* should be made to provide primarily for new residential development and associated local employment and social infrastructure. The area has both good rail and bus links to major local cities and also has a good range of local facilities and services.

A green belt is land that is supposed to be kept free of housing and development – usually to prevent villages and towns growing to the extent that they merge together. For many people it is very important to have green belt land in order to preserve and protect some kind of countryside environment.

The newspaper article finished by urging its readers, the local residents, to protest.

Register your protest and objections now!

A meeting of the council to approve these developments is scheduled for early in January, therefore you need to register your protests and objections as soon as possible – certainly well before Christmas. Letters of protest should be addressed to:

The Senior Planning Officer
Bath and North East Somerset Council
Strategic Policy
Trimbridge House
Trim Street
Bath BA1 2DP

MAKING A CHANGE

Local issues – can young people make a difference?

What do you notice about the two extracts from the newspaper article?

The first extract is written in the technical language of a local council's planning committee – it has numbers and codes that may be meaningless to you. You can probably understand the meaning of it because you know what it is about, but you would probably not read pages of this in order to find the sentence or two that you wanted. How many people would bother to read such material, and where would you obtain copies anyway?

The second extract is urging people to take action in a formal way – a way that should be familiar to you – writing letters of concern and complaint. Letters written to a town planning committee to persuade them against doing something that they intend to do need to be very carefully constructed and considered.

TASK

Think of a local proposal that you might want to protest about. In a group compose an effective letter that will make the local authority think twice about their proposals. You could use the green belt example, or something like a proposal by the local bus company to cancel late night services.

Researching and protesting against an issue like this is difficult for young people. To work to save the local green belt, or to change the planning committee's mind, as in this example, is a difficult and complex activity even for adults. Can young people ever hope to have a real voice in the government of their local communities?

But writing letters of protest does work in the same way that public petitions can work – especially if enough of them are written and sent to the right person! People who rely on elections and votes for their position and power do take notice if enough people contact them about something.

Organisations and protest groups concerned with specific issues are now producing ready-made letters for people to sign and send to the Prime Minister, MPs and local councillors. This is a bid to help members of the public to become involved in issues and is being done for young people too.

Source B A recent Animal Aid protest letter.

Download a protest letter

Animal Aid, an animal rights organisation, has a youth section and often offers downloadable letters on its website. These can then be completed and posted to important people to urge them to take note of the opposition to particular activities, such as fox-hunting. Recent examples have included letters to Prince Charles and The Queen. You can find current examples at: www.animalaid.org.uk/youth

Instructions

To print, click on the Preview button, then choose File, Print on your browser's menu.

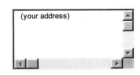

(your address)

June 13, 2002

Dear Mr Hoon

I was most upset to hear that animals continue to be used in weapons tests. This is despite the fact that the Labour Government promised that they would ban such experiments when they got into power.

These experiments are cruel and pointless. The tests involve many different kinds of animals being blasted, gassed, shot and made ill with biological weapons and deadly viruses. I understand that the army are even being allowed to use pigs in shooting experiments, supposedly to help medics understand how to deal with gunshot wounds. How can this be right? Surely pigs' bodies are very different from ours – the military medics aren't training to be vets! Anyway, haven't enough people been shot in the past for us to know what bullets can do?

Animals don't fight wars so I think it is morally wrong to use them in weapons experiments.

Please write to me and let me know what you are going to do about banning these cruel experiments.

Thank you for taking the time to read my letter.

Yours sincerely

(your name)

Factfile

Global letter writing

Amnesty International is another well-known organisation that has protest letter writing as one of its main activities.

- Amnesty International is an NGO – a non-government organisation devoted to aspects of human rights.

- Amnesty International campaigns for political prisoners all over the world – people imprisoned because of their beliefs, views and/or opposition to governments, rather than for criminal actions.

- Amnesty also campaigns against capital punishment and torture.

- One way in which Amnesty works is to organise mass letter writing to the leaders of countries that abuse human rights – keeping them continually reminded that people all over the world care about what is happening.

- Many schools have an Amnesty International group. Forming and running such groups could be one way of completing the coursework section of your course. Look at their website **www.amnesty.org.uk**

- A similar campaign is Drop the Debt, a joint campaign by Christian charities to encourage the world's wealthiest countries to write off the massive and crippling debts owed to them by developing countries. Supporters are provided with ready-written letters to send to world leaders, and by having these to download from their websites, these organisations make it easy for individuals to get involved. See **www.christianaid.org.uk/ campaign/debt**

Political action

←Source C
A petition handover in Downing Street.

→Source D
May Day anti-capitalist protests.

There is a long tradition in the UK of young people of at least student age being involved in protest or political activities to make a difference. This tradition goes back to the mass walks over the moorlands near Manchester in the 1930s to gain public rights to walk over the land.

But it was in the early 1960s that young people really became noticed for taking political action with the annual marches protesting against the stockpiling of nuclear weapons. Although many older people were involved, the CND (Campaign for Nuclear Disarmament) was often thought of as a young people's organisation – and pictures in the press reinforced this. The movement was supported by young people's music in the form of folk or 'protest' songs. These became an important part of the growth of 1960s music, and the Glastonbury Festival began in the 1970s as an event to support CND. Many of our current Labour Party politicians were members of CND in their youth.

Single issue campaigning

Interest and involvement in a particular issue – or single issue campaigning – is a typical way for young people to become involved in the wider world of politics.

Many of today's well-known organisations, such as Amnesty International, began as single-issue pressure groups, small groups – or sometimes just individuals – that began campaigning in very small ways.

Examples of single-issue pressure groups in local community issues are:

- campaign by parents to keep a local school open
- campaign by residents to improve road safety in a locality
- campaign against a local factory that may be polluting the atmosphere
- campaign to raise the awareness of difficulties for disabled people in local facilities.

←Source E
A CND march.

politics & power

Young People Now, May 2001

YPN highlights the experiences of 16-year-old Gemma Smith, a member of Friends of the Earth.

MANY YOUNG PEOPLE get involved in political activity through campaigning groups and political organisations. Gemma Smith actively campaigns with Bristol Friends of the Earth. The group adopted the name CAKE - Constructive Action in a Knackered Environment - and that inspired them to use cakes as part of their campaigning tools. When campaigning on transport issues, they would give a cake to someone who was cycling but not to a single driver in an otherwise empty car. Gemma Smith explains:

"We are all environmentally conscious and if there is anything happening locally that we are not happy about we try and do something about it. We've done local protests such as parades through town dressed up as mutants

protesting against genetically modified organisms. And a community centre used to have a big pile of rubble next to it which we turned into a beautiful community garden."

Ideas for action tend to come from within the group. If something comes up in the news they will discuss it and decide what, if any, action they can take. However they are aware of the limits of working under the Friends of the Earth umbrella, which rules out doing anything illegal. Also as a charity they must avoid any overtly party political involvement.

Gemma knows the limitations, but also the potential, of grassroots action. "A few people can't change the world - unless they dedicate their lives to it," she says.

"and then they're still not likely to make any massive changes. But you can change your local environment - and if everyone put in a little bit of effort we could make the world a better place."

Friends of the Earth groups tend to be locally organised and can determine their own agenda and action points, based on what they see around them. Nationally Friends of the Earth also runs the Youth and Education Network and the Young Campaigners Network.

Gemma Smith is one young person who became involved in political action through a single interest concern that led her and her friends to form a pressure group.

As we can see from this article, Gemma Smith had the help of a larger organisation to support her local activity – in this case the environmental group Friends of the Earth. It is now often the case that all kinds of local issue campaigning can be supported by national pressure groups and organisations. They can provide expert advice, campaign materials and training.

Many national pressure group organisations have specific departments to involve young people, as we have seen with Animal Aid and Friends of the Earth. There are also organisations that exist specifically for the purpose of enabling young people to take part in community action.

←Source F
One young campaigner's story.

A voice for young people

Since the 1960s there has been a growing awareness of the need to involve younger people in decision making and planning. The results of this can be seen in a variety of ways, such as the lowering of the voting age to 18 for the 1970 General Election, and the growing acceptance of young people as members of committees and planning groups by many organisations – including school councils.

The fact that young people are now studying Citizenship in schools is a deliberate act by the government to involve young people in community and global affairs. For this reason the government is also willing to support national and local organisations to help young people to become more involved in their communities.

Obviously the government is not providing the funding to encourage young people to embark on any kind of political protest and action which might be against the government. Rather it is paying to encourage young people to have a voice in their communities and to help improve their communities – it is one way of trying to combat the indifference that young people admit to.

Community action

Town planners and town councils are often faced with this kind of question: How can we provide for the sort of things that young people want and will respect?

Is the answer simply just a skateboard park, or not? Is this a patronising view of what young people want to see in their communities? Can young people think about wider community issues beyond their own interests?

TASK

Devise two lists of needs in your community:

- one for young people in particular
- one for more general age groups.

Remember that needs may not only be specific things such as a youth club. There may be the need for initiatives such as a drugs education programme in the community.

It is obvious that the people who provide and make decisions for communities need to hear the voices of members of the community in order to help them. It is not easy for the voices of young people to be heard in the normal ways of formal public and committee meetings.

Agencies working to help young people find a voice

1. Youth action works!

This is one of the slogans of the Youth Action Network – formerly known as the NFYAA – the National Federation of Youth Action Agencies. This grant-aided organisation has the function of aiding and enabling young people to be effective in all kinds of community action.

Youth Action Network has membership groups in local areas around the UK. Their work includes the training of young people to participate in all kinds of community activities: arranging funding for things that young people may want to do, and working to promote recognition for the things that young people achieve.

These statements describe what the Youth Action Network aims to achieve for young people by encouraging youth participation in community issues:

- Increase young people's understanding of their rights and responsibilities.
- Develop their ability to plan and carry out their own actions.
- Give assurance that young people are not exploited in community participation activities.
- Support young people to take on increasingly challenging activities with increasing levels of responsibility.
- Encourage young people to develop skills to bring about, or resist, change.

TASKS

1. Working with a partner or group, put the Youth Action Network statements in order of importance. Compare lists. Is there a process by which you can arrive at an agreed class ordering of this list?
2. Can you see and explain the difference between an 'adult' attitude that thinks it knows what young people want, and what is best for them, and an attitude that really is on the side of young people? Into which of these categories do the aims of the Youth Action Network fall?

Local issues – can young people make a difference?

The local organisation of the Youth Action Network in Bristol is called Young Bristol Action. A recent project they supported was for a group of young people at a special school to make some improvement to their environment. Young Bristol Action provided project workers to help the group of ten 15-year-old boys to decide what they wanted to do and to help them carry out their aims.

The boys decided that a large wall painting would greatly improve the background to a millennium garden. Young Bristol Action hired a local community artist to assist them and their ideas were turned into a reality.

The project was successfully completed and by a process of reviewing and evaluating their achievement, the boys saw that the skills of teamwork and communication they developed during the work would equip them for future activities in their own and community life.

2. The UK Youth Parliament

The idea for a UK Youth Parliament (UKYP) came from a conference in Coventry Cathedral in May 1996, sponsored by the NSPCC. The UKYP aims to ensure that the young people of the UK are given a voice on any issue that affects them, as laid out under Article 12 of the UN Convention for Children's Rights. It represents an opportunity to be involved in a democratic process at a national and local level – to be listened to by government and local councils. It empowers young people to take positive action within their local communities based upon the issues of concern to them. It is for the young people of the UK to elect, select and decide how the Youth Parliament will operate.

The UKYP is composed of nationwide representatives but also includes established groups such as local youth councils, and individuals. Elections are held on an annual basis, organised in each Local Education Authority (LEA) area.

The UKYP has presented a Youth Manifesto to the Government, the major political parties and service providers for young people. It is intended that these agencies will consider the views of the UKYP when reviewing and creating new policies that will have a direct impact on the young people of the UK.

In some local areas where the Youth Parliament is working successfully – often under the name of Youth Forums – town and city councils are already sending them information about planned local developments, and asking for their opinions and advice.

For further information about the UKYP, and to find out how it is organised in your area contact www.ukyouthparliament.com

Source G
Members of the UK Youth Parliament. ↑

GCSE CHECK

Democracy and the electoral process	Social change and opportunities for groups and individuals to be involved	Role of pressure groups	Your rights and responsibilities as a citizen	Decision making within groups	Problem solving and communication	Finding and understanding specific material	Letter writing for specific audiences

Pressure groups –
how has the animal rights movement campaigned for change?

Aim

You will:

- explore who a pressure group needs to influence in order to achieve national change
- identify and describe the different methods used by a pressure group (the animal rights movement) to change laws and attitudes
- evaluate the advantages and disadvantages of these methods.

Many of the tactics that you examined in the last case study are used by pressure groups in their campaigns nationwide. In this case study you will explore how the animal rights movement has tried to change the ways in which animals are treated using a variety of methods.

↓ Source A

How influencing one target group can influence another target group. This is only a partial picture of how these groups influence each other. You will notice that some arrows go across the diagram to show all of the connections.

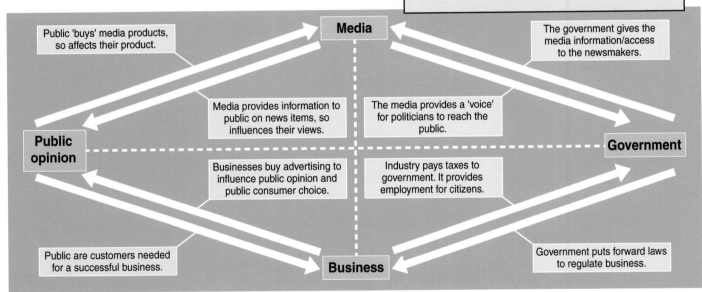

Public 'buys' media products, so affects their product.

The government gives the media information/access to the newsmakers.

Media provides information to public on news items, so influences their views.

The media provides a 'voice' for politicians to reach the public.

Businesses buy advertising to influence public opinion and public consumer choice.

Industry pays taxes to government. It provides employment for citizens.

Public are customers needed for a successful business.

Government puts forward laws to regulate business.

Media

Public opinion

Government

Business

What is a pressure group?

A pressure group is an organisation that aims to achieve a change through pressurising government, business or the media through legal methods of protest and persuasion. When a pressure group is running a national campaign, it needs to influence several groups. We will call them 'target groups'. These target groups can often influence each other. Have a close look at Source A which shows the connections between the different target groups.

TASK

Using information from any of the case studies, explain how the first group can influence the other in each of the examples below:

a) business/industry influences the media
b) the media influences business/industry
c) public opinion influences the government
d) the government can influence public opinion.

How can we fund our campaign?

A. We need money to fund our publicity and campaigns.

B. What about donations or getting sponsorship from a company?

C. Yes, but if we accept sponsorship, can we make sure they are really supporting our aims?

How do we get attention?

A. We need publicity. What's the point of having a campaign, if no one knows about it?

B. How about getting media coverage?

C. Yes, but what kind of publicity will we get? How can we control our image in the media?

How long can we wait?

A. We all know that change is needed.

B. Perhaps we should accept some type of small change. We can push for bigger changes later.

C. Yes, but how long can we wait? Some of our supporters may leave us. Then we'll be back where we started – no support and yesterday's news!

← **Source B**
What questions do pressure groups need to ask themselves?

What do we mean by the animal rights movement?

The animal rights movement is made up of a number of different organisations. All aim to promote the improved treatment of animals, but they disagree on what 'rights' animals have and on the appropriate campaigning tactics to use. Some groups are prepared to work together to achieve gradual change, while others operate alone. Some animal welfare groups co-operate with scientists and other groups argue that all animal experimentation is an abuse of animals.

Some groups or individuals have used threats and acts of violence against property and people to promote their cause. Although the media often describes them as part of the animal rights movement, their use of violence is opposed by many within the animal rights and animal welfare movement as a whole. You need to remember these differences in attitudes when looking at the campaign methods.

What's the priority?

We have seen how a pressure group has to think about how it will influence target groups. However, a pressure group may want to concentrate on one target group more than another. This can depend upon the answers to some key questions that a pressure group may consider before launching a campaign (see Source B).

TASK

In the previous task on page 82, you identified the ways in which different target groups can influence each other. Now, you will be examining the arguments for concentrating upon one of the target groups more than the other.

Choose one of the four target groups identified before: media, Government, public opinion, business. Make a case for the animal rights movement to concentrate on that target group. You will need to consider the effects of your choice on gaining funds (money), publicity and the chance of achieving a change.

Source C
Sir Paul
McCartney

What campaigning methods has the animal rights movement used?

Getting publicity

- Many animal rights/animal welfare organisations use celebrities to attract attention for their cause. Sir Paul McCartney supported the 'Deadline 2000' campaign against hunting with dogs organised by the Campaign to Protect Hunted Animals (CPHA). Celebrities can engage the interest of both the media and the public so that the issue reaches a wider audience.
- Eye-catching demonstrations – groups campaigning against hunting staged several protests that provided news media with shocking or strong visual images that were more likely to be published. Anti-hunt demonstrators dressed as foxes and deer protested outside Parliament, while a model, dressed as a huntsman, 'bathed' in a bath of theatrical blood outside the Millennium Dome.

Economic pressure

- Animal rights groups have targeted companies, such as Huntingdon Life Sciences (HLS), which use animals in the testing of medical drugs and non-medical products. Activists mailed protests to shareholders, directors and staff of companies involved with HLS. Demonstrations were held outside the HLS laboratories and outside the homes of staff and company shareholders. This has affected the willingness of banks and businesses to invest in such research facilities and weakened HLS's share values.
- While peaceful protests outside the laboratories or banks involved with HLS were legal, some activists have been convicted for sending threatening letters to staff (see Source G). In January 2001, the Government unveiled plans to give the police powers to criminalise intimidatory protests outside private homes.

←**Source D**
An anti-hunt
'blood-bath'.

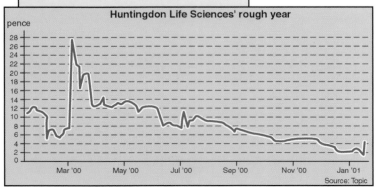

↓ **Source E**
Huntingdon Life Sciences' market value.

Huntingdon Life Sciences' rough year
Source: Topic

Sabotage

- Some animal rights groups disagree with the tactics of the 'Deadline 2000' campaign. Instead of the emphasis on political lobbying, petitions and public awareness campaigns favoured by other organisations, they prefer direct intervention. Hunt saboteurs aim to wreck hunts through sounding horns, laying false trails for the hunt dogs or covering the scent of the hunted animal through strong-smelling products.

Websites and education

- Most animal rights groups have their own website which allows greater communication between the public, the media and the group. E-petitions have been used to secure change. One example is the campaign led by Animal Aid to persuade Oxford City Council to reject proposals for a horse-drawn omnibus. In just seven days the council received 1200 emails from people alerted to this plan from animal welfare web sites.

- National animal welfare groups such as the RSPCA provide education packs, speakers and campaign literature that schools can use, to inform young people of the issues surrounding animal welfare.

Co-operation with the Government and business

- Advocates for Animals is one group which contributes to the Boyd Group, a 'forum for the open exchange of views on issues of concern related to the use of animals in science'. (Advocate for Animals website)

Lobbying MPs

- Many groups are trying to change the law. Animal welfare and animal rights groups try to influence MPs in several ways, such as lobbying (meeting with MPs). Some groups choose a different way as shown in Source F.

Source F

"Anti-hunt campaigners will seek to expose MPs who vote against ...(the) Wild Mammals (Hunting with Dogs) Bill ... A series of advertisements is expected to be placed on Sunday, naming those MPs who supported the Bill and those who did not."

From *The Electronic Telegraph* (27 November 1997)

During 2001 animal rights extremists launched more than 1200 attacks causing almost £3m of damage to property, and individuals have been targeted too.

One scientist, whose work includes experimentation on cats, has been sent letter bombs and razor blades in the post and had his car and house windows damaged.

Extremists also cause harm to wildlife as well, ironically through their attempts to save other animals. Attacks on mink fur farms released thousands of mink into the British countryside but the RSPCA believed the aggressive mink would instead go on to attack local wildlife.

Extremist groups have always represented an unwelcome face of animal rights, particularly for law-abiding animal rights campaigners.

Source G

Animal rights activists target charity shops

"A parcel bomb packed with nails which exploded ... in a charity shop is believed to be the latest in a series of attacks by animal rights activists. The incident comes as a judge ... jailed an animal rights activist for six months after she admitted sending threatening letters to employees of the animal research company Huntingdon Life Sciences."

From *Guardian Unlimited* (1 February 2001)

These charity shops were associated with medical research, including animal experimentation. Some animal rights activists reject any animal experiments, even if it might lead to new treatments.

TASKS

1. Choose two of the campaigning methods shown on these pages and explain how they could affect each of the target groups.

2. Several of the protests shown involve demonstrations outside Parliament or in and around London. What are the advantages and disadvantages to animal rights pressure groups in focusing protest in these locations?

3. Some people would argue that pressure groups should not be allowed to visit or send campaign literature to school. Would you agree? Explain your views.

TASKS

You are a consultant hired to advise animal rights groups who want to stop the use of animals in all experimentation.

1. Look again at Source B, and think about the questions that pressure groups need to answer about their aims and tactics.

   Choose one of the groups below and design a series of tactics to gain publicity for your views. Remember to think about the purpose of the publicity, the need to attract national coverage and how the media might portray your group. You can use the information in sources H, I and J to illustrate your points.

2. Work out how your campaign will pressurise MPs to vote for the option that you want.

3. Your office suddenly receives a preview of the article in Source H. Write a press release indicating your group's response to this opinion poll. Does it change your tactics?

What's your advice?

Group A

A long established, well-known animal welfare organisation with a lot of public donations. It has provided the Government with research in the past and is often included in Government consultations on animal welfare issues. Its charitable status gives the group tax benefits, but means that it could be restricted in campaigning against animal experimentation that benefits humans.

Group B

Totally dependent upon small donations from individuals to survive. It is largely staffed by volunteers, who help to run the office and the website. Many of its members reject tactics of petitions and negotiation; they want a more 'direct' action.

Background

A new government has recently been voted into power, with a comfortable majority. It has promised to allow a 'free vote' on further restrictions on animal testing. This means that MPs will be able to vote freely, there will not be an official 'party' way to vote. The suggested Bill would allow MPs to vote on three options:

i) a total ban on all animal testing in Britain

ii) a partial ban which would allow animal experimentation for medical research only

iii) a continuation of the current rules which allow for testing for medical and non-medical research under licences granted by the Government.

Source H

Majority supports tests on animals

"The use of animals for scientific testing is supported by the majority of adults, according to a Guardian/ICM poll published today. The survey shows that 46% support animal testing and 36% oppose it. ...

The ICM poll shows that 52% of men back animal testing; 31% are against. Women are divided 41% to 41% on the question. The younger generation back an end to testing on animals, even for medicines for human consumption. Out of those aged 18–24, 44% are against such testing, compared to 35% for it. Opposition to animal testing rises to 47%, with 31% against, among those aged 25–34. ...

Conservative voters firmly support the use of animals in scientific testing, with 59% backing such procedures. Labour voters, however, are marginally against by 43% to 41%. ... 45% of Liberal Democrat voters express support for animal testing for medical research with only 35% voting against. ICM interviewed a random sample of 1004 adults aged over 18 by telephone from January 19–21."

From *Guardian Unlimited* (23 January 2001)

Source I

"But figures released yesterday exposed the dilemma for a government that wants to be seen as both animal-friendly and science-friendly. Although the overall number of animal experiments fell slightly, the race to use the new genetics to develop drugs showed in a leap in the use of GM (genetically modified) lab mice and bigger animals like monkeys, cats and dogs. Dog experiments went up 20%, to 8185.

In Huntingdon's massive dog house, … the young beagles live in long, bare, brightly lit concrete rooms, divided up into roofless steel pens. They each get 4.5 square metres of space. They are exercised each day in the long aisle between the pens. For much of the day, gates are opened between the pens and the dogs get to pair off for play. Sometimes staff play with the animals; there are plastic toys in the sawdust on the floor.

After a period of acclimatisation, the dogs are fed medicines and other substances under test – often in the same tablet form, with the same sort of dose, that humans might take. At the end of the study, the beagles are killed and autopsies are done to see what effect the drugs have had on their inner organs.

This week, 17 substances were being treated on the dogs: six anti-cancer drugs, four to treat heart disease, three designed to treat diseases of the central nervous system including one for Parkinson's disease, two for diabetes, one for lung disease and one for a veterinary medicine.

Not all of HLS's work is for UK government medicine requirements. Some is for overseas companies trying to satisfy their regulators; some for weedkiller and fertilisers; some for food additives.

From *Guardian Unlimited* (August 18 2000)

Source J

Animal research statistics

- There were 2.66m tests on live animals in 1998.
- 60% on mice, 22% on rats.
- 52% for medical research and drug testing.
- 34% for biomedical or biological studies.

Source: Home Office

TASKS

1. Copy the 'Least extreme/ Most extreme' line as shown below.

Least extreme   Most extreme

[   ]   [   ]   [   ]

Read these five methods of protest. Where would you place them on this line?

- Dressing up as a fox and protesting outside Parliament.
- Protesting outside a bank which is involved with an animal research company.
- Demonstrating outside a private individual's home who you believe works at a medical research laboratory using animal experimentation.
- Running a website which organises e-petitions against hunting with dogs.
- Sabotaging a hunt.

Explain and share your decisions in a group. You may find that there are different views about the degree of extremism of each method.

2. Think about and debate these statements in a group.
a) 'Animal rights activists are justified in using whatever tactics are necessary to stop animal experimentation, including medical research experimentation.'
b) 'Activists who damage property, or intimidate scientists are damaging animal rights.'

GCSE CHECK

| How pressure groups can bring about change and the methods of protest that they may use | How an individual can take part in a wider campaign and make a difference |

| Justify an opinion and debate issue in the media | Consider other people's ideas |

| Using a variety of sources to construct a reasoned argument |

Have eco-campaigners 'changed the world'?

Aim

You will:

- recognise the global nature of the environmental movement and be able to give examples of its different concerns
- examine and assess the success of the environmental movement in relation to two issues.

Why do we need a global campaign?

In this case study, you will examine how the environmental movement uses tactics to achieve global rather than national or local change.

Environmentalists argue that global campaigns are necessary as the world is interdependent: all of us can be affected by environmental damage and a global response is needed. This map shows this global view in action.

Source A

"Based on current trends, an estimated 34 000 plant and 5200 animal species ... face extinction ... about 45% of the Earth's original forests are gone, cleared mostly during the last century. Up to 10% of coral reefs ... have been destroyed, and one third of the remainder face collapse over the next 10–20 years."

From the United Nations website on bio-diversity (2002)

Montreal 2000

UN Conference agrees to the 'Bio-diversity Protocol', giving countries the right to restrict imports of genetically-modified (GM) foods.

America 1998

More than 140 people die in the hottest month ever recorded in the world. Vice-Climate extremes will continue unless steps are taken to stop global warming.

Peru 2000

The largest rainforest reserve in the world, the Manu Biosphere Reserve, receives money from the new $240 million World Bank fund to protect areas of great biological diversity. In Britain, Friends of the Earth have campaigned against the import of endangered Brazilian mahogany and lobbied major DIY stores – since 1992, imports have dropped by 98%.

↑ Source B
Abseiling protestor and the 'Dracula Corncob'.

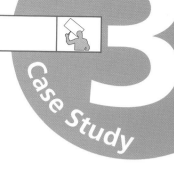
Sellafield, Cumbria 2001

Ireland and Norway protest about the nuclear reprocessing plant in Cumbria. Ireland feared possible radioactive discharges into the Irish Sea while Norway prepared to launch legal action after finding pollution along its coast.

Source C

Britain 2000 "It is now certain that global warming is occurring ... we are in for a period of more extreme weather."

The Association of British Insurers

Tuvalu Island, Pacific Ocean 2001

Rising sea levels lead to evacuation plans. All 31 000 inhabitants will begin moving to New Zealand in 2002. This is blamed on global warming.

Sydney Olympics 2000

Greenpeace developed a spoof website of the Games' sponsor *Coca Cola*. They opposed its use of HFCs, a 'greenhouse' gas. One month later, *Coca Cola* committed to an HFC phase out.

Mozambique 2000

"The reckless human use of fossil fuels ... has helped raise the spectre of climate change. ... By 2025, over half of all people living in developing countries will be highly vulnerable to floods and storms."

World Disasters Report (2000)

TASKS

1. Create a table as shown across a double page. You will be adding to this table throughout this case study. Using the map and Source A, start to insert relevant information. One section has been started to help you.

	Global warming	Endangered species	Other issues
Action issues			
Tactics			Protest on GM foods
Successes			
Setbacks			
Overall view			

2. Using a copy of a world map, draw arrows to highlight the events talked about on these pages that are linked together. For instance, all the events connected to global warming, or things to do with endangered plant or animal life. What does this suggest about the interdependence of global citizens?

Saving the whale, saving the planet?

In this section you will look at two case studies of environmental campaigns. The first concerns the protection of an endangered species, the whale. In order to assess the success of environmental movements, you need to establish your 'criteria for success' – or what you will judge their success against. One way to do this is to look at what the environmental movement itself says is their goal.

Source D

Greenpeace "... is demanding an end to all commercial whaling, once and for all. All whale species must be permanently protected".

From the Greenpeace website

The Whale and Dolphin Conservation Society (WDCS) aim "... to reduce and ultimately eliminate the continuing threats to cetaceans (whales, dolphins and porpoises) and their habitats".

From the WDCS website

Timeline

Some of the main events in the anti-whaling campaign

1975 Greenpeace launches its anti-whaling campaign. This includes public protests, and launching boats which monitor and try to intercept whaling ships.

1979 International Whaling Commission (IWC) establishes the Indian Ocean Whale Sanctuary.

1982 IWC establishes a moratorium on commercial whaling. It does allow 'scientific whaling' (to study whales) and 'Aboriginal subsistence whaling' (whaling by indigenous peoples who have traditionally relied upon whale products for their livelihood).

1983 Convention on International Trade in Endangered Species (CITES) bans the international trade in whale meat.

1986 Most countries have stopped whaling. Before the ban, 13 000 whales were killed every year – 35 a day. Since 1986, Norway and Japan have killed 8000 – just over one a day.

1987 Japan starts 'scientific whaling', killing mainly minke whales.

1993 Norway formally objects to the whaling ban and resumes commercial whaling.

1994 The Southern Ocean Whale Sanctuary is created to protect breeding grounds.

1999 A part of the Mediterranean Sea is declared a whale sanctuary.

1999 Japan and its allies in the IWC block the creation of a South Pacific Whale Sanctuary. Greenpeace conducts campaigns in Japan and Norway to raise awareness of the costs of whaling to the environment.

2001 Britain refuses permission for a Norwegian research ship to operate in British waters fearing it will aid whaling fleets.

2001 WDCS launches the 'Sea Red' campaign due to concern that the ban on trade in whale meat might be lifted. A Greenpeace ship is rammed by illegal Japanese whalers.

2001 "Some 21 airlines, including British Airways, have pledged not to transport blubber or meat from whales as Greenpeace attempts to stop Norway breaking a 15-year ban on exports." From *Guardian Unlimited*

2001 Greenpeace launch a global protest outside Japanese embassies against Japan's Antarctic whaling. Demonstrators wear 'Eyeballs' to show that the world is watching. The IWC votes to continue the ban on commercial trade for one more year.

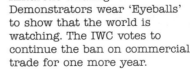

2001 Iceland, a firm supporter of whaling, is refused permission to rejoin the IWC.

2001 It is estimated that whale watching is creating $1 billion a year worldwide.

2002 Japan announces its plan to create a whale farm, to entertain tourists and study breeding behaviour. The plan will involve trapping whales and bringing them into a netted area of nearly two square miles. Environmental groups oppose the idea.

Have eco-campaigners 'changed the world'?

Source E

"Norway and Japan argue that there is no scientific reason to continue the ban on minke and the grey whales, since their populations have returned to healthy levels. There are now thought to be about 900 000 minke whales, roughly the same level as before whaling began, and the total grey whale population is steady at around 20 000 – although the population of Asian grey whales has dwindled to around 100. However, conservationists argue that restarting the legal trade in whale products gives a huge incentive to increase the scale of 'scientific whaling' and will encourage illegal poaching. ...

DNA tests on meat in Tokyo markets have shown that some of it comes from severely endangered species. ... Many species of great whales are still on the verge of extinction. The population of blue whales in the Southern Hemisphere has fallen from 220 000 to just 460, while the population of the right whale has dropped from about 100 000 to 7000."

From *Guardian Unlimited* (9 April 2000)

Source F

"As a conservationist, I say 'Don't whale'. But that's not working. If the IWC can't stop whaling, it has to control it. ... Without a proper management in place at the IWC, ... that would mean a free-for-all ... a completely uncontrolled hunt. ..."

Gordon Shepherd, Director of the International Policy Unit at the World Wildlife Fund (WWF)

Source H

"Captain Paul Watson, heroic environmentalist to his admirers but a ruthless terrorist to his enemies, [sits] upon the silent bridge of the Ocean Warrior ... In 23 years Watson and members of Sea Shepherd, the Vancouver-based group he founded in 1977, have rammed and sank whaling ships, interposed themselves between whales and harpoonists and fought with sealers, loggers and hunters."

From *Guardian Unlimited* (19 July 2000)

Source G

"Japan uses overseas aid to buy support for the resumption of commercial whaling, a senior government official admitted yesterday."

From *Guardian Unlimited* (19 July 2000)

TASKS

1. Add to your table examples of successes and setbacks, tactics and issues for action based on the information on these pages. Look again at the aims of the environmental movement, as shown in Source D. Remember that these can be your criteria for success.

2. Read Source F. What does this show about the environmental movement's success in achieving its aims?

3. Read Source H. This is one example of what is often called an 'eco-warrior'. Write a script for a role-play of a debate between this type of environmental activist and the activist shown in Source F. They are discussing the next steps that the movement should take to achieve success. You might want to think about the following:

   • How do pro-whaling countries persuade other countries to vote with them to end the moratorium on commercial whaling and the ban on international trade in whale meat? (see Source G)

   • What arguments could supporters of a total ban use against the pro-whalers' tactics and arguments? (see Source E and the Timeline)

   • Is it better to allow some commercial whaling and international trade in whale products with controls, than refuse to allow any changes and risk that pro-whaling nations leave the IWC and ignore CITES? (see Sources E and F)

4. On your table, you have an 'overall view' section. Think about the evidence and write your judgement on the success of the environmental movement in protecting whales from whaling. Remember to explain your judgement through referring to the evidence collected.

Clearing the air

"Imagine melting polar icecaps and rising sea levels, threatening ... highly developed coastal areas ... with erosion and storm surges ... Imagine a warmer and wetter world in which infectious diseases such as malaria and yellow fever spread more easily. This is not some distant worst-case scenario. It is tomorrow's forecast."

Kofi Annan, UN Secretary General (2001)

This speech illustrates a major cause of concern of environmentalists – climate change due to global warming. Take a look at the map and graphs below and identify how global warming is estimated to affect the world in your lifetime.

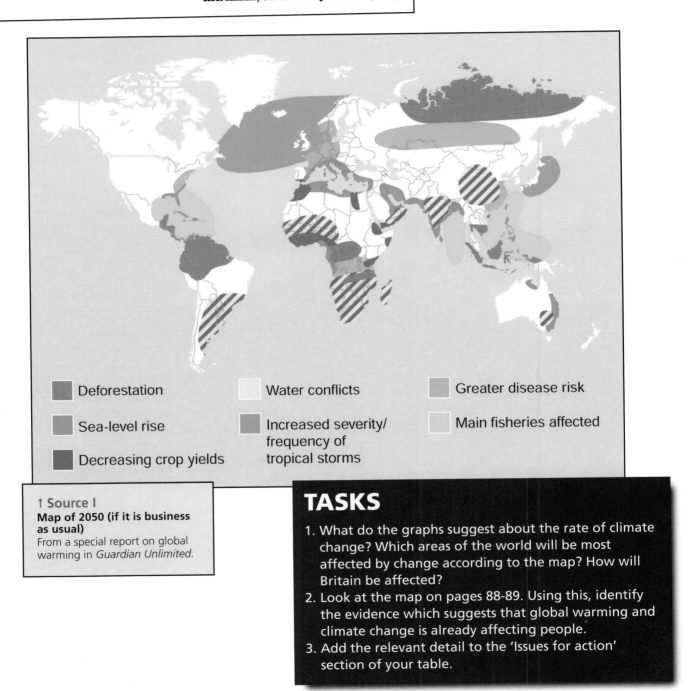

- ☐ Deforestation
- ☐ Sea-level rise
- ☐ Decreasing crop yields
- ☐ Water conflicts
- ☐ Increased severity/ frequency of tropical storms
- ☐ Greater disease risk
- ☐ Main fisheries affected

↑ **Source I**
Map of 2050 (if it is business as usual)
From a special report on global warming in *Guardian Unlimited*.

TASKS

1. What do the graphs suggest about the rate of climate change? Which areas of the world will be most affected by change according to the map? How will Britain be affected?
2. Look at the map on pages 88-89. Using this, identify the evidence which suggests that global warming and climate change is already affecting people.
3. Add the relevant detail to the 'Issues for action' section of your table.

MAKING A CHANGE

What is being done by environmental groups?

At the 1992 Earth Summit in Rio de Janeiro, world leaders recognised the need for sustainable development and for a global response to environmental damage. In 1997, the major industrial nations, along with many developing countries, signed the Kyoto Protocol. This was a first move towards a global strategy targeting global warming. Here are some of its key features:

- The major industrialised nations agreed to reduce greenhouse gas emissions by an average of 5.2% below their 1990 levels within a decade.
- Developing world countries were not expected to meet the same targets as developed countries.

Scientists pointed out that the cuts were small compared to what is needed to avoid climatic instability but it was a first step forward. However America, the single largest producer of CO_2, refused to ratify (or agree to) the Kyoto Protocol. It argued that:

- The Protocol was not the proper way forward and that it would develop its own strategy. Some reports suggested that America had decided not to set targets for reducing its own emissions.
- There was an energy crisis in America and it could not agree to the cuts in emissions without harming its own economy and citizens.
- America was unhappy that developing countries did not have the same targets for cuts in emissions.

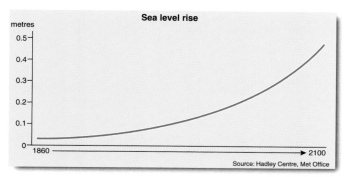

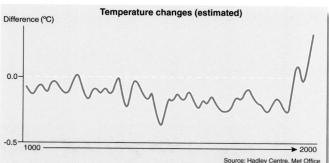

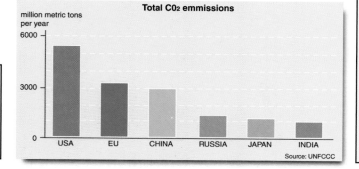

↑ **Source J**
Graphs showing the effects of global climate change.

Factfile

What is 'global warming'?

- Scientists and environmentalists have argued that the polluting effect of industrial and agricultural gases (especially CO_2) have added to the Earth's natural 'greenhouse effect'.

- This effect normally traps part of the Sun's heat and keeps the Earth's surface temperature warmer than it might otherwise be.

- However, with the rise of industrial pollution, the level of the 'greenhouse gases' has risen and therefore the atmosphere is trapping more solar heat.

- The average global temperature increases at a quicker rate than before.

- This 'global warming' is blamed for the melting of glaciers and mountain snow and ice, which contributes to rising sea levels

---

How have environmental groups responded?

Environmental activists worldwide have protested at this setback and have used a variety of tactics to keep the remaining signatories committed to the Protocol. At the same time they have been working with scientists and energy companies to develop and popularise cleaner forms of energy. A commission for 'Wave Power in Scotland' was set up in 2001 to look into this as a possible energy source. Wind farms are increasingly being developed as a source of alternative energy.

↑ Source L
Greenpeace balloon with slogan used in protest about the environmental impact of the Winter Olympics in Salt Lake City, 2002.

Source K

"Following years of campaigning by Greenpeace and other environmental groups, BP announced ... it is dropping plans for the controversial Liberty oil field in Alaska. Greenpeace has opposed this ... on the basis that it will exacerbate (worsen) global warming."

Greenpeace press release (9 January 2002)

Source M

"Electricity production from wind leapt by 31% last year ... according to figures released yesterday ... the use of coal, the main alternative for generating electricity and a major contributor to global warming, fell by 9%."

From *Guardian Unlimited* (10 January 2002)

Source N

In Bonn, 2001 there was a further revision of the Kyoto Protocol.

The attending countries agreed to create new funds to help countries cut down their greenhouse gas emissions, research into cleaner technologies and cope with the effects of global warming. However, environmentalists argued that the new targets for cuts in greenhouse gases were nearly half that required by the Kyoto Protocol.

Source O

Country	% of world population	% of world CO_2 emissions	% of world economy
America	4.6	24	30
EU	6.3	14	23
China	21	13	3.2
India	17	4	1.4

Source P

"Oil giants BP and Shell have joined a Friends of the Earth email campaign pleading with President George W. Bush not to renege (go back) on the Kyoto Protocol climate change treaty. ... So far, 33 000 emails have been sent to the White House. ... At present, 1000 emails an hour are being sent to President Bush.

From *Guardian Unlimited* (3 April 2001)

TASKS

1. Using the sources, write an open letter to the American government and their citizens asking them to recommit to the Kyoto Protocol. Consider the arguments used by America to explain their refusal to ratify Kyoto and think about how you would persuade them to reconsider.
2. Add to your table on the global warming section. Think about the evidence and write your overall view, remembering to refer to the evidence that supports your view.

How successful has the environmental movement been?

You have studied two campaigns led by the environmental movement as well as identifying other issues and tactics. You should have a range of evidence which you can use in the following tasks.

TASKS

1. You are a writer on a newspaper which is going to run a special report on the 'State of the Planet'. Your brief is to write a feature on the success and setbacks of the environmental movement. The working title for this piece is 'Eco-campaigners – saving the world or an endangered species?' Ensure a balanced report, but one that clearly shows your overall conclusion. Consider the following:

   • Identify the successes and the failures of the eco-campaigns.
   • Think about the ways in which environmental awareness is evident in the way that we live our lives.
   • Include striking images to illustrate your feature and capture the reader's attention.
   • You may want to alter the heading in order to convey the tone of the piece.
   • You may have the chance to extend your research through contact with local groups and through websites or media materials.

2. Follow up this story. Make a larger copy of the map on pages 88–89, either for your own use or as part of an 'Environment Watch' display board. As you see news items on the environment, add them to your map. You might want to colour code successes and setbacks so that you can track the impact of eco-campaigns.

3. Think globally; act locally.

   a) Make a large plan of your school. On it, mark how your school promotes environmental awareness.

   b) Identify where there are further opportunities for environmental action. You could include: recycling opportunities, creating habitats to support local wildlife, energy saving and using environmentally-friendly transport strategies.

   c) Expand this to map out the 'environmental health' of your local community. Think about recycling – for example, 'Green Box' schemes. What about the promotion of environmentally friendly transport? Contact the local branch of environmental groups, such as the Friends of the Earth, to identify how they are campaigning for a better environment by thinking globally but acting locally.

→**Source Q**
Protest outside petrol garages against a company regarded by environmentalists as influential in America's refusal to ratify the Kyoto Protocol.

GCSE CHECK

| Provide examples of how groups and individuals can work for global change | Understand the meaning of interdependence and sustainable development | Think of how you could make a difference to your community | Identify a topical issue that you will examine in detail for a coursework |

The wider world

Aim

This section focuses upon 'The Wider World' and by the end of the three case studies you will:

- Start to understand the position of the UK in Europe and internationally
- Analyse the wider issues and challenges of global interdependence and responsibility including sustainable development and Local Agenda 21
- Increase your understanding of some of the key issues affecting the Commonwealth and Europe.

The UK has a central role within the Commonwealth and the European Union – and as a leading figure in world politics it must be actively involved in world affairs.

The Commonwealth

The British Commonwealth of Nations was established in 1931 and was made up of former British colonies and territories which, with the exception of Mozambique, have historical ties to Britain. After India and Pakistan broke away and became independent states in 1947, the Commonwealth was reshaped. Its 54 member states have a total population of 1.7 billion – 30% of the world's population. Even though it has dropped the word 'British' from its name, the British monarch remains the official 'Head of the Commonwealth'.

↓ **Source A**
The 54 members of the Commonwealth.

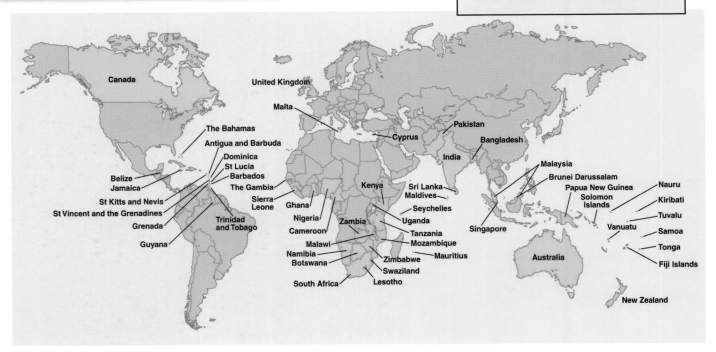

Commonwealth Heads of Government Meetings (CHOGM) are held every two years. Issues relating to human rights and economic and social development are discussed. The Secretariat has responsibility for carrying out programmes agreed upon during these various meetings.

In 1995 the Commonwealth Ministerial Action Group (CMAG) was set up to deal with governments which persistently ignore Commonwealth principles. It can punish members by using economic sanctions or suspension. In 2000 it suspended Fiji following the overthrow of the elected government and in March 2002 it suspended Zimbabwe for a year. The CMAG concluded that the electoral process in Zimbabwe had been 'distinctly flawed'. Despite these actions, it is criticised for having no real power because it does not act as a bloc in international affairs and has little influence over non-members (see Source B).

As well as its involvement in the Commonwealth, Britain is also a member of the United Nations (UN). In 1992 the UN held a conference on Environment and Development in Rio de Janeiro, Brazil. More than 178 governments adopted a comprehensive plan of action to be taken globally, nationally and locally – Agenda 21 (see Source C). This summit marked the first time that development throughout the world was considered with future generations and the planet in mind. It showed that the UN has a major influence at national, regional and even local level.

TASK

1. Look at Source B. What did Prince Charles mean when he said the Commonwealth was 'drinking in the last chance saloon'? In what ways is it 'failing the test'?
2. In groups, try to identify examples of how Local Agenda 21 policy is impacting on individuals and your community. For example, look at food, transport and waste.

Try to make use of interviews, surveys and questionnaires. Draw conclusions about how sustainable your home or school is. Have there been improvements? Use appropriate statistical techniques to record and present your data.

Agenda 21 in the UK

Chapter 28 of the Agenda 21 document calls on local authorities to work with their communities to achieve a local action plan, a 'Local Agenda 21' (LA21). The British government insisted that each local authority should produce its own LA21 strategy by the year 2000 to promote sustainable development within its own area. One authority, Cambridge, in devising its own LA21 emphasised the need for all sections of society to make a contribution (see Source D).

Source B

Before the Commonwealth suspended Zimbabwe in March 2002 the Prince of Wales remarked that the organisation was 'drinking in the last chance saloon'. He said it deserved 'contempt' if it did not stand up for liberal democracy and human rights. The organisation was criticised for 'failing the test' over reports of violence, intimidation and vote-rigging in the Zimbabwe elections.

Source C

Agenda 21 is a 40-chapter document examining world social, economic and environmental issues. It outlines objectives and actions that can be taken at local, national and international levels, and provides a blueprint for nations throughout the world who are trying to adopt forms of sustainable development.

Source D

Cambridge and Local Agenda 21

Work on LA21 began in 1995. At open meetings people had the opportunity to meet with local authority officials and discuss what they valued in the community. Proposals for a sustainable Cambridge were examined.

A strategy was produced and adopted on 9 November 1998. It concentrated on the three Es – Environment, Economy and Equality – and set out a series of suggestions for Cambridge residents. These were points encouraging people to reduce their consumption of water and electricity, go for energy efficient appliances, grow their own vegetables, buy locally produced food and take a shopping bag to avoid being given a new one unnecessarily. The strategy ended with the plea "Local Agenda 21 will only succeed if people like you, your friends, family and colleagues all get involved. As an individual take a few minutes to look at how your lifestyle could be made to be more sustainable".

Britain and Europe – why all the fuss?

Aim

You will:

- understand what the European Union (EU) is and how it is organised
- consider how membership of the EU affects the lives of ordinary people
- understand the attitudes of British people regarding the EU
- analyse media coverage of Britain's relationship with Europe.

Britain has long had links with Europe. Trade has always been important and waves of invaders and settlers have come from continental Europe. Now you are a citizen of Europe and a European Union (EU) made up of 15 member countries and around 375 million people. More are applying to join (see Source A). Since the end of the Second World War, however, Britain has generally been semi-detached from Europe. The famous joke headline 'Fog in the Channel – Europe cut off!' said something real about the attitudes that many British people have towards Europe.

As the British Empire came to an end, British people were unsure about committing themselves to a deeper relationship with European countries (see the Timeline). Some feared a loss of 'sovereignty' and control of some aspects of British economic policies.

Many still worry about further integration and the media often reports and debates the merits of particular European Union proposals.

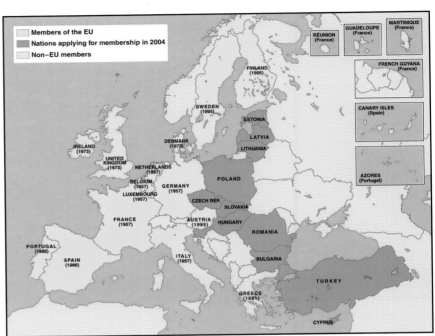

↑ Source A
Map of the European Union with the date of entry of individual countries and the candidate countries (for 2004).

↓ Source B
What do we know about the European Union?

Poll highlights Britons' ignorance over Europe

Millions of Britons are unaware that Britain is a member of the European Union, and one in 15 of the population believe that America is an EU member state, according to the largest government-commissioned survey on British attitudes to Europe. The survey, conducted for the Foreign Office by ICM, reveals that one in five of the population admit they know nothing about the European Union. Europe minister Peter Hain drew encouragement from findings showing that the more people knew about the EU, the more positive they felt. Yet only 75% knew Britain was a member; slightly more knew Germany belonged. Ignorance was strongest among the poor, the young and women. More than one in 10 working class women thought the US was part of the EU.

From *The Guardian* (6 December 2001)

Timeline

1945 There was strong support for the idea of a united Europe as countries tried to avoid repeating the two World Wars. Germany and Italy, which had lost the war, had to be reconciled with France and the Benelux countries (Belgium, The Netherlands and Luxembourg), which had been occupied by German soldiers. Countries looked for ways that they could co-operate – both politically and economically. The European Coal and Steel Community was formed.

1957 Six countries signed the Treaty of Rome which set up the European Economic Community (EEC) or Common Market. Britain decided not to be involved.

1960s British requests to join the EEC were turned down by the French President Charles de Gaulle in 1961 and 1967. Britain was part of another organisation at this time – the European Free Trade Association – which included Britain, Austria, Denmark, Norway, Portugal, Sweden and Switzerland.

1973 Britain was finally allowed to join the EEC and this was confirmed by a referendum of the British people in 1975 (the EEC by now had nine members).

1979 Launch of the European Monetary System, or exchange rate mechanism (ERM) which attempted to bring EU countries' economies closer together.

1987 Introduction of the Single European Act which led to the Single Market in 1993. This means goods from one EU country can be moved to another EU country without paying a tariff (tax).

1992 Treaty of Maastricht – this set a timetable for monetary union between the EU countries and agreed some common social and working rights across EU countries. Britain 'opted out' of some of these changes for many years.

1997 Treaty of Amsterdam – this established a clearer idea of European citizenship and also specified the link with national citizenship: "Citizenship of the Union is hereby established. Every person holding the nationality of a Member State shall be a citizen of the Union. Citizenship of the Union shall complement and not replace national citizenship".

2002 The 'Euro' replaced the national currency in 12 European countries but Britain was not one of them. The decision on whether Britain would join the Euro would be made in a later referendum.

Source C

British youth 'most ignorant' about EU

British youngsters are more ignorant about, and have lower expectations of the EU than others of the same age in every other member state, according to a poll published today. *Eurobarometer*, the European commission's polling arm, shows that Britons in the 15–24 age group are not well informed about their rights to:

- move permanently to any EU country
- work in any EU country
- access health care and social welfare
- study anywhere in the EU.

Nearly a quarter of the Britons polled were unable to say what being a citizen of the EU meant. A total of 28% thought the EU was 'a way to create a better future for young people'. But the UK figure was just 7.9%. … Average 'don't know' rates for the poll were 9.5%, but 26.9% in the UK. … British ignorance could be explained in part by the UK's failure to take part in a EU-wide TV information campaign designed to educate citizens about their rights.

From *The Guardian* (8 November 2001)

TASKS

1. Draw at least three conclusions about the European Union from the map. Look at who joined when, and think about how and why the EU is getting larger.
2. What does the Timeline indicate about British attitudes towards closer European integration?
3. Write a 250-word critical commentary on the two newspaper articles from *The Guardian* reporting the apparent ignorance of British young people and the wider population about European issues. Use evidence from all of the information in this case study to support your commentary.

What is the point of the European Union?

Why have 15 countries joined together to become the European Union? The EU provides a framework of law and institutions to allow economic and political co-operation. Together the EU aims to:

- promote economic and social progress
- assert the identity of the EU internationally
- introduce European citizenship
- develop an area of freedom, security and justice
- maintain and build on established EU law.

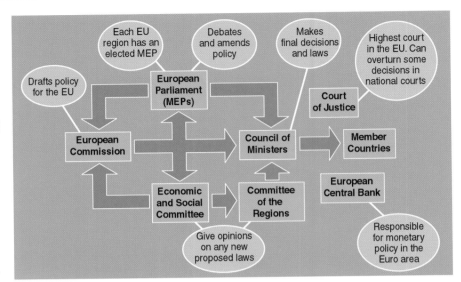

↑ Source D
The structure of the European Union showing its various institutions.

Another of the aims of the EU is to reduce inequalities between the people who live in its member countries. The rich industrial areas continue to develop at a faster rate than the poorer areas – countries like Greece and Portugal are much poorer than the Netherlands or Germany. Through its Regional Fund the EU gives money to encourage companies to build new factories in poorer areas. There is also a Social Fund to assist areas where, for example, there is high unemployment.

Achievements of the EU

- The EU has provided a free trade framework for Europe's prosperity since the Second World War.
- It has helped to maintain peace and co-operation between the member countries.
- It has provided a clear path forward for countries emerging from political dictatorship and, in Eastern Europe, centrally planned economies under the control of communist leaders. For example, the EU helped Greece, Spain and Portugal turn their back on dictatorship. And it is the hope of EU membership that is now driving political and economic reform across Eastern Europe and the Balkans.
- The European institutions (see Source D) have enshrined fundamental rights as a general principle of European law and have developed legislation on freedom of movement within the EU.

Many European politicians are keen to try to bring European institutions closer to the public and encourage greater participation by ordinary people in EU affairs. EU laws affect all areas of the lives of its people – the air they breathe, the water they drink, the food they eat and the things they buy.

←Source E
The EU has a blue flag system to recognise and reward clean beaches.

TASKS

1. Do you agree with the general aims of the EU? What would you change or add?
2. a) Look at the Factfile and choose what you think are the five most important benefits that Britain gains from membership of the EU. Justify your choices.
   b) How would people who oppose further European integration respond to the various points in the Factfile? Select and argue against at least one point from each of the five sections.

Britain and Europe – why all the fuss?

Factfile

What does Britain gain from membership of the EU?

1. It can be argued that membership of the EU has transformed the British economy.

- In 1973, when Britain joined the EU, 35% of exports went to other EU countries. By 2000, the share had risen to 57%. Exports to the rest of the world also rose – but more slowly than exports to Europe.
- It is estimated that up to 3.5 million British jobs depend on exports to the EU.
- Britain receives the largest share of inward investment into the EU – partly because it is a gateway to the European market. American firms employ almost 1 million people in Britain.
- With 376 million people, the EU is the world's largest consumer market, giving British people access to lower prices and more choice.

2. Membership of the EU has impacted on many areas of British society.

- Britain will receive £10 billion of EU structural funds from 2000–2006 to aid development in poorer regions of Britain.
- British women have the right to receive pay equal to men because of an EU agreement.
- The EU has introduced new rights for part-time workers, most of whom are women.
- EU rules mean British workers have the right to a maximum 48-hour working week.
- European police co-operation is helping to crack down on terrorism, drug trafficking and organised crime.

3. The single market seeks to guarantee standards of consumer protection in the EU and increase competition.

- British citizens are guaranteed rights similar to their UK statutory rights whenever they buy anything throughout the EU.
- Package tour operators have to meet certain advertising criteria thanks to EU rules. If they change your holiday or cancel it they must provide compensation.
- Cheap airlines such as *EasyJet* and *Ryanair*, which have introduced low cost air travel within Europe, would not have been possible without the EU liberalising the air market.
- Car safety rules are being introduced across the EU, including rigorous crash tests to ensure cars meet high standards of protection.

4. EU agreements mean that British people have a cleaner and safer environment.

- The Treaties of Maastricht and Amsterdam have enshrined commitments to sustainable development and environmental protection in EU law.
- Britain has cleaner water, cleaner air and cleaner beaches because of action taken at EU level. EU rules prohibit the discharge of toxic substances into EU waters. Sea pollution around the UK has been reduced through EU action to stop dumping of raw sewage at sea. European law protects holiday beaches from pollution. A decade ago half of British bathing beaches failed to meet EU standards, today over 95% meet them.
- Since 1992 an EU directive means that all new petrol driven cars are fitted with catalytic converters.
- Since 1972 the EU has taken more than 200 measures to protect the environment.

5. There are benefits for young people and education.

- Britain is eligible for up to £2.9 billion of EU funds from 2000–2006 to fund education and training.
- In 1999, 10 000 UK students in higher education studied in another EU country.
- Since 1995, over 830 000 young people from across the EU have studied, trained or worked in another member state with support from EU education, training and youth programmes.
- The right to free movement in the EU means that 100 000 British people are working in other member states at present.

Source: the pro-European organisation Britain in Europe

Britain, Europe and the media

Inaccurate or partial stories in the media undermine our right to a clear and factual understanding of Britain's place in the EU. However, the politicians are quick to complain when elements of the media do not see issues and events in the same way as they do!

←Source F

Front page from *The Sun* (November 1990) Jacques Delors was President of the European Commission at the time. He had just published a report which recommended a Single European Currency. The Conservative government strongly opposed these plans and *The Sun* shared these doubts. Delors was described as 'the Froggy Common Market Chief'.

Source G

"A significant part of the media does not treat with any real objectivity the issues of Europe. The media that is not opposed to Europe often remains cowed by the force of the anti-European propaganda; or follows lamely the same agenda. We always seem to be on the receiving end of European initiatives, never their instigators. Europe always appears to be trying to shape us, rather than the other way round. The British way of life always seems to be in peril in one way or another. Our fisheries decimated. Our agriculture distorted by subsidies. Foreigners seem to be fiddling with the details of our national life and interfering."

Tony Blair (July 1999)

↑ **Source H**

The Euro arrived in January 2002 but with what consequences in Britain?

Source I

"What sort of EU do parts of the British media foresee in 2010? An EU in which jackbooted Eurocops roam the streets of Britain, arresting anyone eating bent bananas or drinking beer in pints. A Europe where lollipop ladies are harmonised, where darts are banned from British pubs and where rubber ducks are banned from the great British bathtub. All of which, and more, have passed recently through the pages of our press. Euromyths provide great fun for journalists. The media has a mission to entertain. And some of them rise magnificently to that goal. But they are failing in their other mission to inform. That is the conclusion we must draw from a recent *Eurobarometer* survey which showed that just 2% of the British people believe what they hear about Europe in the media."

Robin Cook, then British Foreign Secretary (November 2000)

Arguments against further integration between Britain and the EU: is the EU taking us over?

There are many organisations and pressure groups – over 50 – who oppose either aspects of, or all of Britain's relationship with the European Union. Public opinion polls show that a large proportion of the British people are unenthusiastic or even downright hostile to co-operation with the European Union (although the results vary depending upon the phrasing of the question which is asked). Its activities are sometimes seen as a threat to British ways of life and some EU regulations do not always suit the UK.

Case Study

"Britain has the world's fourth largest economy. While trading links to the EU are important, the UK is strong enough to keep its own currency and therefore its democracy. No one in Canada is seriously considering the adoption of the US dollar despite the fact that the country exports 85% of its goods to America. Personally I'd rather join an Anglo-Saxon union of Britain, America, Australia, New Zealand and South Africa than any European union – perhaps involving the Scandinavian countries, where English is widely spoken as well. If we are afraid for the jobs of our workers, it might be well to remember that for every person in the EU, there are another 19 who are not. Why can't we sell our products to the rest of the world, which has much more to offer us than Europe?"

"I'm British not European – I want to hang on to our own customs and traditions. I don't want unelected bureaucrats in Brussels telling me how we should be living in this country. We need to keep our independence. In many parts of the world such as Eastern Europe we are seeing democratic power being returned to the people. The EU seems obsessed with trying to achieve further political and economic integration even though many of the cultures and peoples are vastly different. A country which does not have its own currency and which no longer manages its own money supply is not a country anymore, but a province."

"I love French wine, I like going on holiday to Europe but we're not talking about getting on well with Europe here. At present the wealthier nations such as the UK, Germany and France all pay more into the EU budget than they get back. If we integrate further, we might need to pay more to support poorer countries at our own expense. The people running the EU will want everything to be equal. Also, if further members from the former Eastern Bloc join, this will make the problem worse. There is not enough wealth in Western Europe to support any quick development of the new Eastern European members. How can we fail to learn the lessons of the collapse of the Soviet Union (or even nearer home, the pressure for Irish or Scots independence)? Artificial unions of countries do not work and eventually break up in chaos."

TASKS

1. Over a period of a week scan a range of magazines and newspapers for references to Europe and the European Union. Make a class display of these stories. What conclusions can you draw from the press coverage?

2. The European Commission's Press Office in London monitors the British press's coverage of the EU. It has uncovered many 'Euromyths' – scare stories based on hearsay, rumours and half-truths. Look at their website http://www.cec.org.uk/press/myths/index.htm

   a) Do you agree with Source G that "… a significant part of the media does not treat with any real objectivity the issues of Europe"? Give at least three reasons for your answer and some examples.

   b) If so, why do you think that this is the case?

3. Using Source C and the talking heads above, make a list of the reasons why some people in Britain are dissatisfied with British membership of the European Union and unhappy about proposals for further integration measures in the future.

4. Write a 150-word reply disagreeing with one of the sets of views outlined in the talking heads. The Factfile (see page 101) will give you some ideas.

Britain, the EU and the future

There will be many issues for both Britain and the European Union to resolve in the coming years. The EU is far from perfect. Some of its institutions and key policies have been recognised as needing reform for many years, for example:

- The small numbers of people turning out to vote in European elections right across Europe does not indicate much enthusiasm for the work of the European Parliament (in Britain the figure is only one third of the electorate). It is seen as a talking shop which does not achieve very much. And the European Commission itself has the impression of being rather bureaucratic, distant and undemocratic.
- The Common Agricultural Policy was designed to ensure that Europe was self-sufficient in food and to maintain stable prices for farmers. However, it was designed over 40 years ago and led to high subsidies (support payments) for inefficient small farmers and has contributed to the creation of butter mountains, wine lakes and farmers being paid not to plant certain crops. Nearly half of the EU budget is devoted to agriculture.
- The whole of the EU will have to cope with the political and economic consequences of enlargement as EU membership expands, particularly in eastern and south-east Europe. This will lead to changes in the way that decisions are made and will mean that richer countries like Britain, Germany and France will effectively need to subsidise the economic development of countries such as Poland, Hungary and Slovakia.
- The British people and politicians will need to make up their minds on a wide range of issues including:
  - How far does Britain see itself as a European country or does it want to follow a slightly different path from its continental neighbours?
  - Should Britain lose some 'sovereignty' and control over its currency and the management of some of its economic and foreign policies?

↑ Source J
The European Union Flag adopted in 1986. Against the background of blue sky, twelve golden stars form a circle, representing the union of the peoples of Europe. The number of stars is fixed, twelve being the symbol of perfection and unity…

↓ Source K
Many sports and entertainment competitions are organised on a European basis, such as the Champions League in soccer and the Eurovision Song Contest. Why do you think that European competitions like these are so popular?

You may not feel it at the moment, but you will have a voice (albeit a small voice) in answering some of these questions in the future. Citizens of the EU should get involved and try to understand the complex forces that affect their daily lives.

The EU and youth

The EU offers support for young people across Europe in a number of ways, for example:

- it promotes exchanges between countries by providing advice, training and funding
- it helps with work opportunities through providing information on job vacancies, general employment and living conditions, residence permits and essential documents required when travelling abroad.

Britain and Europe – why all the fuss?

After enlargement to a total of 27 countries, the EU will have some 75 million people aged 15–25. The EU acknowledges that 'due to this fact, the Union has to pay attention to the needs and opinions of young people in Europe'. In 2001 it produced a report (called Youth White Paper) based on extensive consultation in all member countries including Britain. The British Youth Council carried out the largest consultation of young people in the UK to date, issuing over 200 000 questionnaires through associations, youth councils and even rock concerts. It also held a conference. These were some of the findings.

Having your say and Europe

- Neither the survey nor the discussions suggested that young people in the UK are as sceptical about the EU as the media portrayal of the population at large. Young people, however, simply do not have enough information about what the EU does to make informed decisions.
- Over a quarter of respondents said that they did not know whether the EU was important in their lives and a large number of survey respondents – 41.9% – said that they thought the EU had no effect on their lives.
- The importance of the Internet for information dissemination came through strongly. Discussion groups criticised the reliability and accuracy of much of the information presented to them at present. The lack of such information in schools and other public places was criticised.
- Europe was seen as having power chiefly in the areas of trade, human rights and equality – and these areas were felt to be beneficial. The power of the EU structural funds to regenerate deprived areas was seen as very positive.
- Several participants placed the collective power of the EU in the context of globalisation, and the need for EU countries to work together to tackle global problems collectively seemed to be acknowledged. One consistent area, however, where the EU was seen negatively, occurred in a perceived 'corruption' of national and regional culture and identity.
- Young people wanted to see further reform of the EU. For example, the role of the European Parliament was felt to be too slight – as was the visibility of MEPs.

Adapted from *Listening to the Unheard*, British Youth Council (2001)

TASKS

1. Write a letter to your MEP suggesting ways in which you feel that the organisation of the EU could be improved and be more closely connected to the concerns of people in your locality.
2. Try inviting him or her to your school to be questioned by class representatives. UNICEF provides useful free materials to help you to 'Put it to Your MP' – these include activities, draft letters and even model press releases! Look on their web site www.unicef.org.uk
3. Working in pairs, create a poster to convince the large proportion of young people in Britain who feel that the EU has no effect on their lives that they are mistaken.

GCSE CHECK

UK's relations in Europe and with the EU	What the EU is, how the UK is involved and the impact of EU decisions on British citizens	Express, justify and explain in writing a personal opinion relating to Britain and Europe	Use imagination to consider other people's experiences and be able to think about, express, explain and critically evaluate views that are not their own

Developing countries – should richer nations help them?

Aim

You will:

- develop an improved understanding of the role and operation of various relief agencies
- consider the 'debt problem' and gain an appreciation of the human costs involved
- examine the debate regarding the benefit of giving aid to poorer countries.

Poverty is about hunger. Poverty is about lack of shelter. Poverty is being sick and not being able to see a doctor. Poverty is not knowing how to read and not being able to go to school. Poverty is not having a job, fearing for the future, living one day at a time. Poverty is losing a child to illness brought about by unclean water. Poverty is powerlessness, lack of representation and freedom.

Poverty is a situation that people want to escape from. It is a call to change the world so that many more may have enough to eat, adequate shelter, access to education and health, and protection from violence. Importantly, people must have the ability to voice concerns and have a say in what happens in their communities.

Poverty has many dimensions. It has to be looked at through a variety of indicators such as income levels and consumption, social indicators, and indicators of vulnerability to risks (see Source A).

→Source A
Measuring global poverty: people living below $1 a day in developing countries (1987, 1990 and 1998).

	Number of people living on less than $1 a day (millions)		
Regions	**1987**	**1990**	**1998**
East Asia and the Pacific	417.5	452.4	267.1
(excluding China)	114.1	92.0	53.7
Eastern Europe and Central Asia	1.1	7.1	17.6
Latin America and the Caribbean	63.7	73.8	60.7
Middle East and North Africa	9.3	5.7	6.0
South Asia	474.4	495.1	521.8
East Asia and the Pacific	217.2	242.3	301.6
Total	**1,183.2**	**1,276.4**	**1,174.8**
(excluding China)	879.8	916	961.4

Source: Global Economic Prospects and the Developing Countries (2001)

Developing countries – should richer nations help them?

One of the main aims of the leaders of the world's richest nations is to reduce the proportion of people living in extreme poverty in developing countries. Secretary-General of the United Nations, Kofi Anan, said tackling world poverty was one of the priorities for the UN in the Twenty-first Century. He asked world leaders to commit themselves to halving the number of people living in absolute poverty by the year 2015.

In most regions poverty rates have shown some decline (see Source B). The greatest number of poor people live in South Asia, but the proportion of poor is highest in Sub-Saharan Africa, where civil conflict, slow economic growth, and the spread of HIV/AIDS have left millions barely surviving. In East Asia, however – especially in China where an open economy has boosted living standards – poverty rates have declined fast enough to meet the goal in 2015. Most other regions could achieve the goal, if economic growth continues and income distributions do not worsen.

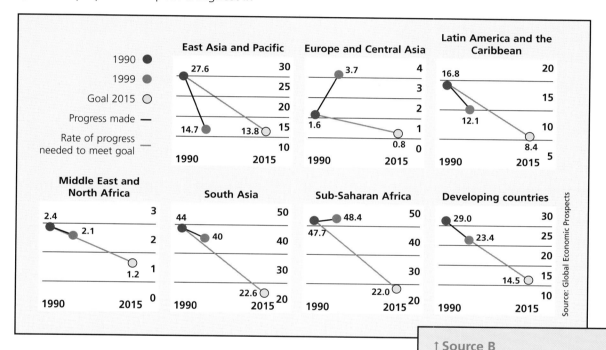

↑ **Source B**
Global poverty rates are down 20% since 1990, but progress is very uneven (poverty rate = % below $1).

TASKS

1. From your reading of the text, briefly explain why there has been a significant decrease in poverty rates in China while Sub-Saharan Africa has seen an increase.
2. Look at Source A.
   a) Which region has seen the sharpest fall in numbers between 1987–1998?
   b) Which regions have seen a rise in numbers between 1987–1998?
3. Now consider Source B.
   a) In which regions have poverty rates between 1990–1999 worsened?
   b) Which region appears to have made the most progress in reducing poverty rates? Briefly explain your answer.

Income is not the only measure of poverty. The poor lack education. They suffer from malnutrition and poor health (see Source C). They are vulnerable to natural disasters and crime, and they lack any sort of political freedom and power. In a world where 1.2 billion people live in extreme poverty, ensuring a sustainable future for the poorer nations is crucial (see Source D).

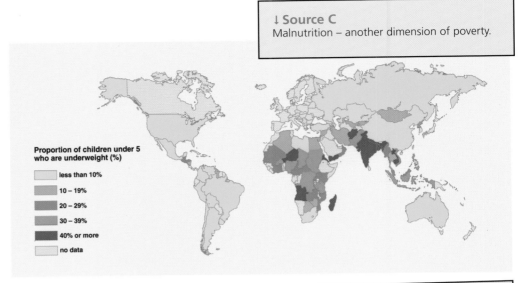

↓ Source C
Malnutrition – another dimension of poverty.

Proportion of children under 5 who are underweight (%)

- less than 10%
- 10 – 19%
- 20 – 29%
- 30 – 39%
- 40% or more
- no data

↓ Source D
Sustainable or unsustainable future?

UNSUSTAINABLE

Traditional methods of 'progress' focus on economic growth and ignore the fact that some people benefit:

- at the expense of others
- at the expense of the environment
- at the expense of future generations.

Such notions of 'progress' promote practices which are unsustainable both in the short and long term.

SUSTAINABLE

By contrast the notion of sustainability emphasises:

- increased levels of social and economic wellbeing for all, especially for the least advantaged
- increased emphasis on protecting the environment
- that future generations should inherit as much 'wealth' as we ourselves inherited.

Poorer nations increasingly need foreign aid from wealthy countries such as the UK to make it possible for poor people to increase their incomes and to live longer, healthier and more productive lives.

Based on wealth, the world can be divided into:

- More Economically Developed Countries (MEDCs) which include the richer, more industrialised nations of the so-called 'North'.
- Less Economically Developed Countries (LEDCs) which include the poorer, less industrialised nations of the so-called developing 'South'.

The wealth of a country is measured by its gross national product per capita – its GNP per person. The GNP per capita refers to the total value of goods produced and services provided by a country in a year, which is then divided by the total number of people living in that country. To make calculations easier, when comparing different countries, the GNP is normally given in US dollars (US$). Statistics can be misleading but it is hard to argue when so much evidence seems to bear out the huge inequality of wealth between the MEDCs and the LEDCs (see Source E).

Source E

A cure worse than the disease

"Everybody knows that the world isn't fair. Inequality is part of the human condition. Always has been, always will be. What has never really been clear is just how unequal life is. Now, thanks to an economist at the World Bank, it is clear. The richest 50 million people, huddled in Europe and North America, have the same income as 2.7 billion poor people. The slice of the cake taken by 1% is the same size as that handed to the poorest 57%."

Larry Elliott, *The Guardian* (21 January 2002)

Developing countries – should richer nations help them?

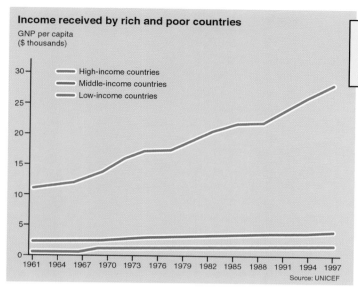

Income received by rich and poor countries

GNP per capita
($ thousands)

- High-income countries
- Middle-income countries
- Low-income countries

Source: UNICEF

←Source F
Income received by rich and poor countries.

One way to help LEDCs develop and improve their living standards is to give them 'aid'. Aid is a practical way of giving resources such as money, food, goods, technology or specialist help – for example, medical. The basic aim in giving aid to an LEDC is to help develop its economy and services, which in turn will improve the standard of living and quality of life of the people who live there. It can be given in two main ways:

- The first is as short-term aid – this helps to solve immediate problems. For example, bringing help quickly to people affected by disasters and emergencies such as volcanic eruptions, famine and war.
- The second is long-term aid – the aim of this type of aid is to improve basic living standards and help people make better use of their own resources. Long-term aid should help a country progress and improve its level of development.

There are many reasons why the LEDCs need aid. Generally they fall into three broad categories:

- To try to improve the standard of living. This often requires receiving or borrowing money for large development schemes such as building an international airport or improving hospital facilities.
- Many countries need to receive or borrow money in order to buy goods from the MEDCs. Unfortunately, by borrowing money, these countries often fall further into debt.
- Many LEDCs suffer as a result either of natural disasters (for example, flooding, drought, earthquakes) or human-caused disasters (for example, war and desertification – the spread of desert into areas which were well vegetated).

←Source G
Life under the burden of poverty and debt – flood victims in Mozambique wait to be fed.

TASKS

1. a) What is the difference between an MEDC and an LEDC?
   b) What is GNP? How is GNP per capita calculated?
   c) What is the difference between short-term and long-term aid?
2. Draw at least three conclusions from the world map about the distribution of children under five who are underweight.
3. Do you agree with Larry Elliott when he writes "Inequality is part of the human condition. Always has been, always will be. What has never really been clear is just how unequal life is"? In your answer, try to give reasons why people today are far more aware of the poverty facing many populations throughout the world.

There are basically three types of aid:

1. **Bilateral aid** – Here resources are 'given' directly by a wealthy 'donor' country (MEDC) to a poor 'recipient' country (LEDC). Often the aid is 'tied', meaning that certain conditions are imposed. For example, if money is given to a country for an important building programme, the donor country can insist that the building contract must be given to them, increasing its trade. Meanwhile, the recipient country falls further into debt because it will have to repay the loan and it cannot give the work contract to its own building companies.

2. **Multilateral aid** – This is when the richer countries give money to organisations such as the International Monetary Fund (IMF), the EU Development Fund or the World Bank, who then redistribute the money to the poorer countries. There should be no political conditions or ties but quite often these organisations will hold back the aid if they disagree with the recipient country's economic and/or political system. In the Declaration of the South Summit in April 2000, richer countries were urged to dedicate a minimum of 0.7% of their GNP to Official Development Assistance (ODA). This figure is rarely reached (see Source H).

3. **Voluntary aid** – Voluntary organisations raise money from the general public in the richer countries for use on specific projects in the poorer countries. There are no political ties. These organisations are normally the first to provide essential resources like food, clothing and shelter following major disasters.

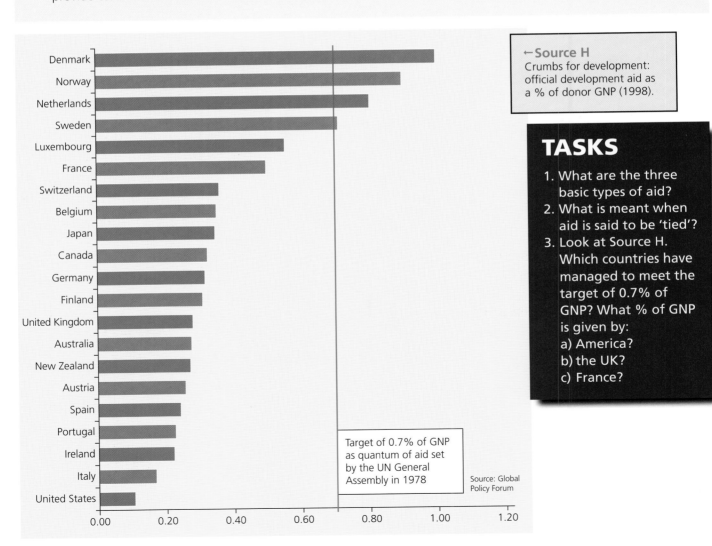

←Source H
Crumbs for development: official development aid as a % of donor GNP (1998).

Target of 0.7% of GNP as quantum of aid set by the UN General Assembly in 1978

Source: Global Policy Forum

TASKS

1. What are the three basic types of aid?
2. What is meant when aid is said to be 'tied'?
3. Look at Source H. Which countries have managed to meet the target of 0.7% of GNP? What % of GNP is given by:
   a) America?
   b) the UK?
   c) France?

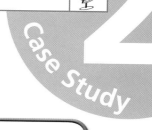

Organisations fighting for world equality – some of the main 'players'

Who are they?
International campaign for debt relief, succeeding the International Jubilee 2000 campaign.

Activities
'Protest can make a difference.' Its global campaign has moved debt relief from being a marginal issue to global attention.

Who are they?
Britain's largest organisation dedicated to campaigning on third world and development issues, with over 10 000 supporters and 120 active local groups.

Activities
Lobbying decision-makers, campaigning on aid, arms sales and genetically modified (GM) food, researching and fundraising.

Who are they?
Founded in 1942. A confederation of 12 non-governmental organisations working together in more than 80 countries to find lasting solutions to poverty, suffering and injustice.

Activities
Funds many development projects, provides emergency relief in times of crisis and campaigns for social and economic justice.

Who are they?
A programme of the New Economics Foundation and the official successor organisation to Jubilee 2000 UK.

Activities
'We are a think-and-do tank.' It provides up-to-date accurate analysis, news and data and promotes effective campaigning and action.

Who are they?
Development charity created by the British and Irish churches in 1945.

Activities
'We believe that it is our duty to address the causes of poverty. Many of these causes, such as debt or trade, are essentially political or economic in origin.' It funds a large range of development projects and campaigns.

Who are they?
Catholic development and relief agency helping people in poverty in the third world to access resources needed to become self-reliant.

Activities
Helping people in England and Wales to understand causes of poverty, and challenges the government and international organisations to make sure their policies work.

Campaigners who want to see the crippling burden of debt repayment eased say there is no better time to wipe the slate clean and offer poor countries a fresh start.

Some people, however, are concerned that corruption in developing countries can undermine the case for debt relief. A Christian Aid report recognised that donors are less willing to contribute cash to poor regions if they fear money will only end up in the pockets of local officials. Corrupt heads of state in some developing countries have stolen billions of pounds from aid budgets, either stashing the money away for their own use or using it to buy arms or finance other illegal activities. The report also pointed out that corruption is not limited to developing countries. In recent years several governments including those of Germany, France and the UK have been involved in bribery and corruption scandals.

Developing countries – should richer nations help them?

The initial amounts borrowed by these poorer countries have disappeared into new loans. The pressure of repaying these loans and huge amounts of interest has forced many countries to reduce their funding for essential public services such as health and education. The cost, according to Jubilee Research, is in human lives.

Despite all the efforts of very worthy voluntary organisations and campaigns led by celebrities such as Bono, Muhammad Ali, Sir Bob Geldof (the founder of the 1985 Live Aid) and world leaders like Pope John Paul II and the ex-President of the USA Bill Clinton (see Source L), most LEDCs continue to struggle to repay a fraction of what they owe. For the LEDCs their debt total rises £1566 per second!

How much would debt cancellation cost?

Spread over 20 years, the cost of cancelling the debts of the 52 Jubilee 2000 countries is only one penny a day for each person in the industrialised world.

Source: Unfinished Business, Jubilee 2000 report

Who pays who?

For every £1 in grant aid to LEDCs, more than £13 comes back to the MEDCs in debt repayments.

Source: Global Development Finance (2001), based on 1999 figures for grants and total debt

Every day in 1999, $128 million was transferred from the poorest countries to the richest in debt repayments. Of this, $53 million was from East Asia and the Pacific, $38 million from South Asia and $23 million from Africa.

Source: Global Development Finance (2001), 1999 figures for lowest income countries

Developing countries often end up paying much more back than they originally borrowed. Costa Rica borrowed less than £4 million from Britain in 1973. By 1999 it had paid Britain more than £7 million of that loan but still owed more than £1 million.

Source: House of Commons Hansard Written Answers (10 June 1997)

Source I
"When we get the Pope and the pop stars all singing on the same sheet of music, our voices do carry to the heavens. … Global poverty is a moral affront, and confronting the challenge is simply the right thing to do."
Bill Clinton

Bono and Muhammad Ali.

The human cost of debt

Even after receiving debt relief under the Heavily Indebted Poor Countries (HIPC) initiative, Mali's debt repayment was $88 million in 2000. This is greater than the level of government spending on health ($54 million in 1998), in a country where one in four children do not live to see their fifth birthday, and where per capita spending on health is $5 as compared to the World Bank's recommended level for basic health care of $12.

Sources: Halfway There?, UN Human Development Report (2000); Oxfam International position paper (July 1999)

Due to the HIV/AIDS crisis, life expectancy in Zambia is expected to drop from 43 to 33 years, a level last experienced in Europe in medieval times. Over half a million children are out of school, and these numbers are not declining. Yet debt service after enhanced HIPC still remains more than spending on health and education in 1998 combined.

Sources: Decision Point document; Halfway there?, UN Human Development Report (2000); Oxfam International position paper (July 1999)

If debt had been cancelled in 1997 for 20 of the poorest countries, the money released for basic healthcare could have saved the lives of about 21 million children by the year 2000, the equivalent of 19 000 children a day.

Source: UN Human Development Report (1997)

For each additional 1% of GDP spent on health and education, child mortality is reduced by 24%. In 1999 Zambia paid $438.5 million in total debt service, 13% of GDP. If this money had been invested in Zambian healthcare, child mortality would have been reduced from a rate of 20% to only 0.8%, the same rate as in America.

Sources: Global Development Finance (2001) debt service; under-five mortality rate from UN Human Development Report (2000)

TASKS

1. Over a period of a week scan a range of magazines and newspapers for references to poverty throughout the world. Make a class display of these stories. What conclusions do you draw from the press coverage?
2. In the campaign against world inequality do you think the involvement of well-known individuals helps? Give reasons for your answer.
3. Write a 250 word critical commentary report on 'World inequality – why we must act'. Use evidence from all of the information in this case study.

GCSE CHECK

Opportunities to bring about change internationally	UK relations with the Commonwealth and UN	Global interdependence and responsibility	Analyse information from different sources	Consider other people's experiences

Why should British citizens be involved in world affairs?

Aim

You will:

- start to understand the important part that the UK plays on the 'world stage'
- gain an appreciation of the role that the UK plays in organisations such as NATO, the IMF and the WTO
- examine the debate regarding globalisation and fair/unfair trade.

NATO

NATO – the North Atlantic Treaty Organisation – is the world's most powerful defence alliance. Its aim is to 'safeguard the freedom, common heritage and civilisation' of all its members by promoting 'stability and wellbeing in the North Atlantic area'.

There have been 53 UN peacekeeping missions between 1948–2000, with 40 of those taking place since 1990.The UN is also credited with ending more than 170 conflicts by negotiating settlements (see NATO Timeline).

Some people believe that the UK should not be so involved in world affairs, but the majority accept that as a 'superpower', the UK has responsibilities extending far beyond national boundaries.

The answer to the question 'Why should British citizens be involved in world affairs?' is simple – we might be citizens of Britain but we are European and world citizens as well.

NATO Timeline

1949 Twelve states – Belgium, Canada, Denmark, France, Britain, Iceland, Italy, Luxembourg, the Netherlands, Norway, Portugal and the America – sign the North Atlantic Treaty in Washington DC.

1950 US General Dwight Eisenhower is appointed supreme NATO commander.

1952 Greece and Turkey join the alliance.

1955 West Germany joins NATO; the Soviet Union and eight Eastern European states respond by forming the Warsaw Pact.

1967 NATO's new headquarters are opened in Brussels.

1982 Spain joins NATO.

1990 NATO and Warsaw Pact states sign the Conventional Armed Forces in Europe treaty (CFE) and publish a joint declaration on non-aggression.

1991 Warsaw Pact is dissolved; NATO sets up the North Atlantic Cooperation Council as a forum for consultations between NATO members, East European states and the former Soviet republics.

1992 NATO supports peacekeeping activities in the former Yugoslavia.

1993 NATO agrees to offer former Warsaw Pact members limited associations with the alliance in the form of the Partnership for Peace programme.

THE WIDER WORLD

Why should British citizens be involved in world affairs?

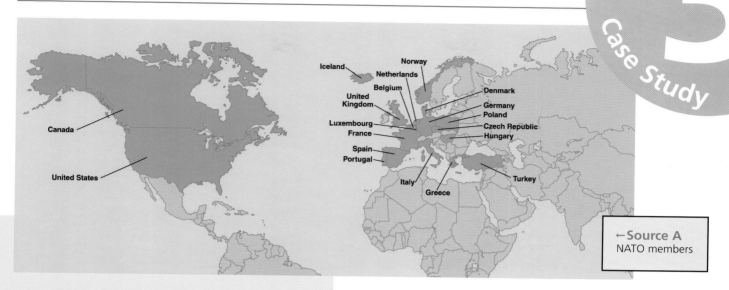

← Source A
NATO members

1995 NATO embarks on its first ever military operation to force the Bosnian Serbs to negotiate a peace settlement; NATO deploys thousands of troops – the Implementation Force (Ifor) – to monitor and enforce a ceasefire in Bosnia.

1997 Ifor replaced by a smaller force called the Stabilisation Force (Sfor); NATO and Russia sign the Founding Act to establish a framework for security cooperation.

1998 NATO-Russia Permanent Joint Council set up to give Russia 'a voice but no veto'.

1999 Three more countries – the Czech Republic, Hungary and Poland – become the first former Soviet bloc states to join NATO, taking the alliance's borders some 400 miles towards Russia; NATO begins an 11-week campaign of air strikes against Yugoslavia over Kosovo without United Nations approval.

2001 NATO undertakes disarmament operations in the former Yugoslav republic of Macedonia.

2002 Addressing a meeting in Bucharest for ten aspiring member states, the American Deputy Secretary of State, states that the USA wants to see NATO admit as many new members as possible.

After World War I the power of the British Empire began to decline but even today, the UK has many responsibilities towards its former territories. During the last century the UK established a 'special relationship' with the major world superpower – America. Crises like World War II, the Gulf and Bosnian wars and the 'war against terrorism' saw the two countries draw closer still. Apart from America, the UK had more peacekeeping forces serving in the Afghanistan and Gulf wars than any other NATO member.

As well as being a founder member of the United Nations and member of the European Union, the UK is also actively involved in other world organisations which are committed to peacekeeping, upholding human rights or helping poorer nations, such as in Sierra Leone.

TASKS

1. Look at the information on NATO and choose what you think are the two most important benefits for Britain from membership of NATO. Justify your choices.
2. Over a period of a week scan a range of magazines and newspapers for references to NATO activities. Make a class display of these stories. What conclusions do you draw from the press coverage?
3. Working in pairs, create a poster to convince the large proportion of young people in Britain who feel that NATO has no effect on their lives that they are mistaken.

World poverty

Famine, disease, civil war and a failure of aid programmes has left the number of those living in absolute poverty at 1.2 billion people in 2000, the same as in 1990. In 1995, at a United Nations conference on social change, countries pledged to halve world poverty by 2015. To achieve this aim, the UK agreed to donate 0.7% of its GNP to ODA. In 1997 only 0.26% of GNP was spent on aid. By 2001 this had increased to 0.31% and the Labour government expects this to increase to 0.33% by 2003–2004. This amounts to a 45% increase in aid spending since 1997, but in the opinion of many people, it is simply not enough.

In 2000 the UK was the fourth largest donor, giving $4501 million (about £3007 million) out of the global total of $53 billion (see Source C).

Public opinion polls in the UK have consistently shown strong support for helping poorer countries. Yet, the percentage that the UK spends on international aid remains well below the European average. If increases continue at this rate, it will be 40 years before the UK reaches the 0.7% target.

The World Trade Organisation

The World Trade Organisation (WTO) is the policeman of global trade. The WTO's decisions are absolute and every member must obey its rulings. The extra powers given to the WTO are supposed to ensure that disputes are settled according to international trade principles, and avoid a situation where a powerful country might try to take advantage of a weaker one.

The WTO has 141 members and all decisions have to be agreed by all members. Decisions can only be reversed by a unanimous vote, just as they can only be made that way. Given the large number of members and the fact that no country can use a power of veto, it is never very easy to sort out trading problems.

The details of how much countries are prepared to cut tariffs and trade barriers are hammered out at trade rounds which are lengthy sessions of talks. Not everyone is happy with the work of the WTO and increasingly it finds itself criticised.

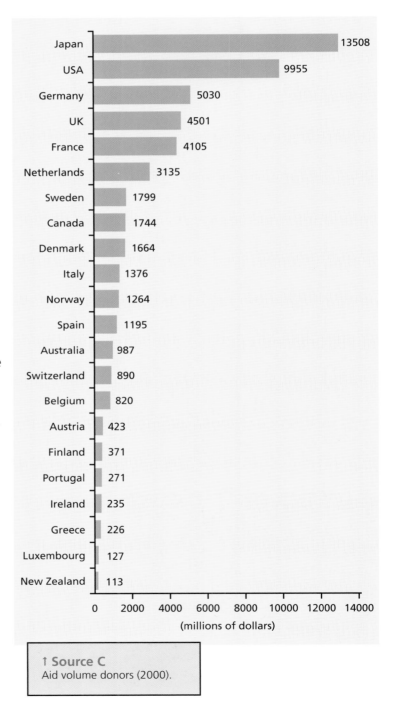

↑ **Source C**
Aid volume donors (2000).

> **Source B**
>
> The four aims of the WTO:
> 1. Making trade more competitive by removing subsidies.
> 2. Expanding trade concessions to all members.
> 3. Establishing freer global trade.
> 4. Making trade fairer by establishing rules.

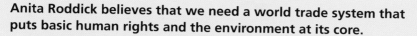

Anita Roddick believes that we need a world trade system that puts basic human rights and the environment at its core.

"Here's a question for the world trade negotiators. Who is the system you are lavishing so much attention on supposed to serve?

According to the WTO, we don't have the right to discriminate between tuna caught without killing dolphins and tuna caught by those who don't care, don't worry and don't try.

According to the WTO, the livelihoods of the small-scale banana farmers of the Windward Islands are worthless – now facing ruin as the WTO favours the big US exporters.

The truth is that the WTO, and the group of unelected trade officials who run it, are now the world's highest court, with the right to overturn local laws and safety regulations wherever they say it 'interferes with trade'.

… The truth is that 'free trade' was originally about the freedom of communities to trade equally with each other. It was never intended to be what it is today. A licence for the big, the powerful and the rich, to ride roughshod over the small, the weak and the poor.

Internationalism means that we can see into the dark corners of the world, and hold those companies to account when they are devastating forests or employing children as bonded labour. Globalisation is the complete opposite, its rules pit country against country and workers against workers in the blinkered pursuit of international competitiveness.

… Businesses which forego profits to build communities, or keep production local rather than employing semi-slaves in distant sweatshops, risk losing business to cheaper competitors without such commitments, and being targeted for take-over by the slash-and-burn corporate raiders, reinforced by the weight of the WTO.

The rules have got to change. We need a radical alternative that puts people before profit. We must start measuring our success differently. If politicians, businesses and analysts only measure the bottom line – the growth in money – then it's not surprising the world is skewed. It's not surprising that the WTO is half-blind, recognising slash-and-burn corporations but not the people they destroy.

… Measuring what really matters can give us the revolution in kindness we so desperately need. That's the real bottom line … By putting our money where our heart is, refusing to buy the products which exploit, by forming powerful strategic alliances, we will mould the world into a kinder more loving shape."

Anita Roddick's address to the International Forum On Globalisation (27 November 1999)

TASKS

Imagine you are a journalist listening to Anita Roddick's speech.
a) Write a 150-word report for a news agency which sums up her views.
b) Write a 150-word response to the speech from the viewpoint of the WTO.

→ **Source D**
Trading with principles – Anita Roddick, founder of *The Body Shop*.

In her speech Anita Roddick talks about putting people before profit. Globalisation appears at times to do the opposite, putting profit before people. Critics of globalisation say that the gains of the MEDCs have been at the expense of the LEDCs. An example of this can be seen in the world coffee trade. When global coffee prices fall, this can have a disastrous effect on small-scale producers in LEDCs. Many are forced into debt while others may lose their land and their home.

According to Oxfam, millions of coffee farmers in LEDCs are living in extreme poverty while 'big businesses' in the coffee industry continue to make record profits. Oxfam is concerned at the growing disparity of wealth between different parts of the coffee industry, following a 60% drop in the value of the crop on international commodity markets in the last three years.

→Source E
Worlds apart! Coffee farmers seem to be losing out as, in the trading pits of the Coffee, Sugar and Cocoa Exchange in New York, the future value of coffee is changing hands.

Rich versus poor

Oxfam says that, in real terms, coffee prices are lower than they have ever been. The value of raw coffee beans has fallen sharply due to overproduction, but prices paid for the processed coffee in consuming nations have remained much the same. Oxfam believes that this is having devastating consequences for poor farmers in coffee growing countries. Meanwhile, the charity says, big multinational food companies and cafe and restaurant chains have gained enormously from the drop in prices.

Oxfam says the price of raw coffee exported from producer countries is less than 7% of the price paid as a consumer in the West – the rest goes to coffee processors and retailers in rich countries. Oxfam points out that *Nestlé* – the giant Swiss instant coffee processor – and the fashionable American coffee shop chain *Starbucks* have steadily increased their profits.

In its first reaction, the British Coffee Association (BCA) said it shared Oxfam's concerns over low prices for producers. However, the BCA – which represents coffee manufacturers selling in the UK – says Oxfam "fails to address the fundamental economics of the coffee market in the long term".

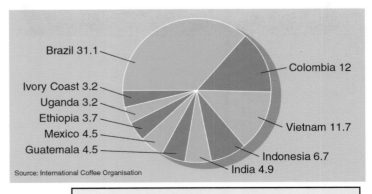

Brazil 31.1
Colombia 12
Ivory Coast 3.2
Uganda 3.2
Ethiopia 3.7
Mexico 4.5
Guatemala 4.5
Vietnam 11.7
Indonesia 6.7
India 4.9
Source: International Coffee Organisation

↑ Source F
Annual coffee production (in millions of 60kg bags).

Ethical trading and Fairtrade

The Fairtrade Foundation ensures a better deal for producers in LEDCs. It was set up by CAFOD, Christian Aid, Oxfam, Traidcraft Exchange and the World Development Movement. Farmers who grow Fairtrade certified coffee work in co-operatives and agree to abide by certain environmental and ethical standards.

In 2002 the *Starbucks* coffee chain, followed the *Costa Coffee* chain in the UK by selling Fairtrade endorsed coffee in the UK. *Starbucks*, which reported record profits of $805 million in the three months to the end of December 2002, buys about 1% of the global coffee crop. The Fairtrade Foundation stated that the move would provide a higher profile for certified coffee and benefit the environmental movement, even though the amount sold would be small. A *Starbucks* spokeswoman said, "We are committed to this kind of initiative, we're delighted to have been able to sign this agreement, it's not just advertising".

Despite this move, critics insist that coffee chains like *Starbucks* are only responding in a very small way to public demand from its British customers. *Starbucks* profits continue to rise as world coffee prices continue to drop.

The coffee trade is just one of many examples where the wealthier countries benefit at the expense of the poorer ones. In the UK, pressure groups have campaigned to adopt ways of tackling the issue, through 'ethical trading' (or 'sound sourcing') and 'Fairtrade'. It is important not to confuse the two approaches – while they complement each other, each one aims to assist different groups of people in different circumstances.

Thanks to a lot of media coverage on the working practices of companies such as *Nike*, *Adidas* and *GAP*, which have set up factories in developing countries, there is a growing awareness amongst British people about the ways in which these workers are exploited. Ethical trading targets its efforts at improving the working conditions of these employees. Its objective is to work with employers to ensure basic human and working rights – to develop and improve on safe and decent working conditions and general standards of living.

TASKS

1. What do you think helped to change the attitudes of *Starbucks* and the *Costa Coffee* chains in choosing to sell Fairtrade endorsed coffee?

2. Use the Fairtrade website www.fairtrade.org.uk to present a 250 word report on its 'Production Standards and Conditions' and/or its 'Terms of Trading'.

3. In pairs, or in a group, try to discover if stores in your local area sell products bearing the Fairtrade mark. Note down what types of products they are – for example, coffee, tea, bananas, snacks, chocolate, cocoa and so on.

4. What do you think Source E tells you about what you have been reading on world inequality?

5. 'Charity begins at home'. Some people believe very strongly that the government should be spending money on improving poverty in the UK rather than giving money to international aid. Do you agree? Give reasons for your answer using evidence from all of the information in this case study.

GCSE CHECK

| Opportunities to bring about change internationally | Global interdependence, responsibility and sustainability | Consider other people's experiences | Analyse information from different sources |

Media

→ Source A
Press protest over 'gagging'.

Aim

This section focuses upon the 'mass media' and by the end of the three case studies you will:

- be able to give examples of the different types of media
- consider how difficult it can be to live in an 'information society'
- analyse the power of the media in creating and influencing opinion
- start to understand why the media is 'gagged' on occasions.

The mass media is the term used to describe all the possible ways of communicating to a large number of people at the same time. It includes newspapers, magazines, radio, television, cinema and the Internet. Some of it is visual, some printed and some auditory – often it is a mixture of all three.

The mass media is part of our everyday lives. It provides information, entertainment, ideas and opinions. For the majority of people, their knowledge of what is going on in the world and the view they have of events is shaped and presented to them through the mass media.

As a result of the speed of technological advances, the power and influence of the media in the Twenty-first Century are steadily growing. Internet use in the UK has grown; the numbers of homes connected to the Internet in 2001 was 10 million – up from 6 million a year earlier. Source B shows the importance of this Internet growth in detailing the amount of time individuals devote to it.

Source B ↓

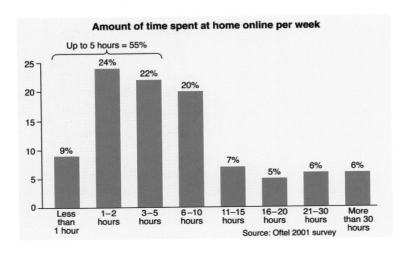

Amount of time spent at home online per week

Up to 5 hours = 55%

Less than 1 hour	1–2 hours	3–5 hours	6–10 hours	11–15 hours	16–20 hours	21–30 hours	More than 30 hours
9%	24%	22%	20%	7%	5%	6%	6%

Source: Oftel 2001 survey

% of age groups who use the Internet

Age group	% Male	% Female
15–24	51	49
25–34	45	48
35–44	52	54
45–54	43	48
55–64	30	34
65–74	18	13
74+	3	4

TASKS

1. Keep a diary of your television viewing during a full week. Make a note of the different types of programmes you watch, for example soap operas, sport or cartoons. Construct a table to show your findings and comment on these findings.

2. Look carefully at Source B.
   a) What is the percentage of people using the Internet for more than five hours per week?
   b) Who do you think would use the Internet for over 30 hours per week?
   c) What percentage uses the Internet for more than three hours a day?
   d) Were you surprised that the 35–44 age group was the highest Internet user? Why?

Source C

The power of television

"Many other forms of the media such as television, radio and newspapers also continue to have an important influence in our lives. The Internet has failed to change television viewing habits, with new figures showing that we watch more television than ever before. Europeans now spend more than three hours a day watching television and viewing has risen in every European country. On average the British watch just over 3.5 hours per person per day.

In the last three years, the number of people using the Internet has grown from a European average of fewer than one in ten, to more than one in three. Those in Northern European countries are the highest users of the Internet, while those in warmer European countries are less addicted. In Scandinavia over 50% of the population are regular users. In the UK 49% of the population use the Internet. But only 12% and 11% of Spanish and Italians respectively describe themselves as 'regular' users.

Britain, however, has lost its position as the best-read country in Europe. Ten years ago Britain had Europe's highest national daily newspaper circulation figures, with 40.5% of the population reading a paper every day.

By 1999 that figure was down to 31.4%. Often the need to attract a larger circulation results in a 'dumbing down' in the quality of the content produced by the media. Newspaper circulation figures confirm that the majority of consumers prefer the tabloids (popular press) to the broadsheets (quality press).

People today are exposed to more channels of communication than ever before. With the arrival of widespread digital technology, you will be able to exercise more control of what, when, and how you receive your information. We are already starting to see this with interactive television. Increasingly digital technology will be used as a marketing tool, to communicate with the individual consumer on a personal level. As a viewer you will soon have the power to block what you don't want to see on your screen."

Adapted from an article, 'Brits come out top in TV watching league' in *The Guardian* by Claire Cozens (Tuesday 20 March 2001).

TASKS

1. Why do you think the highest users of the Internet are Northern European countries?
2. What does the phrase 'dumbing down' mean in the passage above?

How **powerful** and **influential** are *different* types of media?

Aim

You will:

- demonstrate knowledge of the power of the media in putting across different views
- explore some of the theories concerning the power and influence of the media
- appreciate how topical issues are portrayed in the media.

The media has had to change rapidly due to innovation and the pace of technological development. The first British newspaper was produced in 1702 but it was only when more people could read that the power and influence of the newspaper really began.

Newspapers today are generally divided into 'tabloid' (popular press) or 'broadsheet' (quality press). Often the tabloids are smaller in size with a large number of pages covering main news stories in Britain. They often include what are called 'human interest' stories – stories about well-known people, tragic accidents and scandals. Broadsheets are larger in size, covering main news items from across the world. Broadsheets often include supplements that contain specialist topics and reports.

Broadsheet (quality press)	Tabloid (popular press)
Generally appeals to the reader wanting: • balanced information on a variety of topics and issues • international news items • specialist sections, such as finance and politics • to spend a good deal of time reading it.	Generally appeals to the reader wanting: • entertaining news, such as the private lives of celebrities • simple layout • plenty of images • easy read • summary of news, not in-depth analysis.

↑ **Source A**
Tabloid or broadsheet – what's the difference?

→ **Source B**
Newspaper circulation figures. Tabloid papers are in red, broadsheet papers are in blue.

Source: Audit Bureau of Circulations (2002)

Daily newspapers

Title	Overall daily circulation
The Mirror	2 081 814
Daily Star	773 823
Daily Record	561 990
The Sun	3 351 419
The Express	876 470
Daily Mail	2 384 573
The Daily Telegraph	954 509
The Financial Times	468 268
The Guardian	389 543
The Independent	194 940
The Times	672 507

Sunday newspapers

Title	Overall daily circulation
News of the World	3 992 320
Sunday Mirror	1 732 154
Sunday People	1 311 526
Sunday Sport	214 746
Sunday Express	873 078
Mail on Sunday	2 360 652
Independent on Sunday	190 634
The Observer	435 194
The Sunday Telegraph	742 755
The Sunday Times	1 405 357
Sunday Mail	622 991

Media coverage

Media coverage of certain news items and events will vary a great deal depending on editorial policies. For example, some broadsheets are reluctant to cover gossip stories about celebrities, whereas certain tabloids devote a lot of space to these. Quite often a newspaper will support one political party and some of its articles might be biased towards this party. The same piece of news in another paper might be reported very differently.

The way in which a story is presented can affect the way an audience responds. Rather than merely giving the facts, newspapers – and the tabloids in particular – are often accused of using emotive language. This is language that appeals to the emotions and often makes use of strong visual images.

TASKS

1. Examine Sources A and B.
   a) Which daily newspaper is the highest-selling tabloid?
   b) Which Sunday newspaper is the highest-selling broadsheet?
   c) What is the circulation figure for the daily tabloids? Work this out as a percentage of the number of papers sold every day.
2. In pairs or small groups, look at the headlines set out here. Each pairing refers to the same news story. The first headline is from a tabloid, the second one is from a broadsheet.
   a) In what ways is the reader being influenced or led into an opinion by the headlines?
   b) What effect does the choice of words like, 'batters', 'Mummy' and 'agony' have?

"MUMMY HAS BLOOD COMING OUT OF HER NECK
– I don't want Daddy to kill Mummy"
Girl's agony as cop batters family

'There will be no divorce – the only way out is death,' police officer warned wife before attack.

ANIMAL FANATIC HORNE DIES IN HUNGER STRIKE
Jailed bomber refused doc's help

Animal rights activist dies after hunger strike

DR BOTCHER DEATHS TO BE PROBED BY CORONER

Struck-off surgeon could face criminal inquiry

Other media

Radio remains popular and is still a powerful medium. The invention of radio in the late-Nineteenth Century, and its growth in popularity during the Twentieth Century allowed people to have far greater access to information. Radio is called an 'auditory' medium because the listener depends entirely on sound.

Television

Unlike newspapers, television can broadcast news stories almost as soon as they break. The leading item is regarded as the most important, but the priority of the stories might change as more news items come in during the day. Quite often the importance attached to some news stories changes from channel to channel, depending on the 'target audience' and according to the time of day.

As well as these traditional forms of the media, the Internet has an increasingly powerful impact on people's lives. As more homes are linked to the Internet, the 'information superhighway' across the world is accessible in seconds.

There are many moral issues that arise from the activity of the media and quite often they overlap with each other (see Source D). The issue of censorship is looked at more closely in Case Study 2.

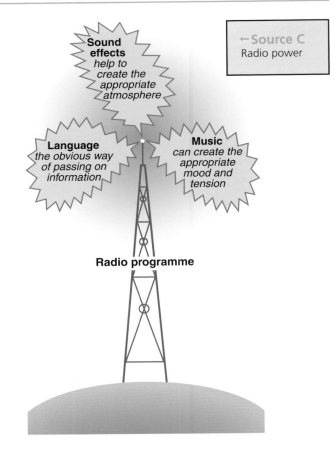

Sound effects help to create the appropriate atmosphere

Language the obvious way of passing on information

Music can create the appropriate mood and tension

Radio programme

← Source C
Radio power

Source D

Moral issues stemming from the media

- Advertising
- Censorship
- Legislation
- **Moral Issues**
- Accountability
- Bias/propaganda
- Ownership/influence
- Press Reporting

TASK

Conduct a survey of people aged 11–14, 15–18, 19–30, 31–40, 41–50 and 50+. Ask each group the following questions:
a) Which different forms of the media do they use?
b) How long do they devote each week to each mass media form?
c) What are the attractions of each of the mass media?
Present your findings in written and graph form.

Press reporting

There are numerous ways in which the media can influence public opinion, attitude and behaviour:

- language and writing style
- reporting methods
- headlines and particular images used
- editorial comments
- news item selection, scheduling and positioning
- ownership interference and political bias.

On 11 September 2001 a terrorist attack was carried out on the World Trade Centre in Manhattan, New York. People found themselves gasping in horror as they watched endless replays of the destruction of the Trade Centre Twin Towers. Television images showed us the people caught up in the chaos and terror of the events. The Internet transmitted reports and images within seconds. On the next day newspapers sold out as people rushed to read the story in detail.

The headlines were quite clear – 'Apocalypse', 'Declaration of War' and 'Doomsday America' (see Source E). The language, style and images chosen by the various forms of the media left the readers in no doubt about the horrific nature of the attack. This story dominated television, radio, newspapers and the Internet.

Many television networks made the decision to broadcast commercial-free news coverage. Why do you think the networks stopped showing commercials? As the story unfolded, newsroom and newspaper editors faced some difficult decisions about whether or not to show graphic images of the victims of the attack. Thousands of people perished, and there were many images available showing some of them dying. This raises important questions for each reader and viewer:

- Should these images have been shown on television or was that in bad taste?
- Should these images have been shown in newspapers or was that in bad taste?
- What guidelines should television and newspapers use when deciding which images are suitable to show?
- When does showing the images of someone's death become bad taste?

TASKS

1. It was reported that certain songs were removed from some American radio station playlists as a result of the attacks. These included:
   It's Raining Men – Geri Halliwell
   Burning Down the House – Talking Heads
   Rock the Casbah – The Clash
   Beds are Burning – Midnight Oil
   I Would Die for You – Prince
   What a Wonderful World – Louis Armstrong.
   a) Do you agree with the actions of the radio stations?
   b) What songs would you have removed from the list of banned songs? Why?

2. Video the news on BBC1, ITV and Channel 4 on the same night. Watch each and note the differences in coverage of any one same story and note which stories are carried by some channels but not others. Suggest reasons to explain the differences in news coverage.

3. As a group, produce two newspaper front pages – one tabloid, one broadsheet – on two of the following topics:
   - a train crash
   - a terrorist act
   - animal rights protest
   - the marriage of a celebrity.
   You must decide on the following:
   a newspaper title; a headline; a sub-heading; a date; an image and the wording of the report.

← Source E
Newspaper headlines from 11 September 2001.

A great deal of power and influence lies with different types of media and, importantly, with the individuals who own them. An American writer, Frank Vogl, stated, "It has often been said that journalism's role is to afflict the comfortable and comfort the afflicted. Sadly, too many media owners – many of whom have great power – see the role of the media differently: they believe the role of the media is to comfort the comfortable and ignore the afflicted."

Ownership and influence

Some owners of newspapers and television networks have great power and influence. In a recent survey, a panel of media analysts selected Rupert Murdoch, the founder of *News Corporation,* to top a list of influential figures (see Source F). *Microsoft* co-founder Bill Gates was number two. The panel said that Murdoch had a 'unique power' over the UK media sector and was 'much reviled, often feared and grudgingly admired'.

In 2001 Mr Murdoch's *News Corporation*'s turnover was £16.5 billion and employed over 34 000 staff. The company has a large stake in *Twentieth Century Fox* and owns 23 American television stations and cable and satellite operations in Australia, China, Europe and Latin America. It also owns a third of *BSkyB*, the UK's leading satellite television provider, as well as *News International*, which produces *The Sun*, *The Times*, *The Sunday Times* and *The News of the World*.

There is no doubt that people in powerful positions in the media can sometimes put forward their own political viewpoints or use the media to present their own views on particular issues. Many people believe that the success of New Labour in the 1990s was partly thanks to Rupert Murdoch's support in *The Sun*, which previously had been recognised as being anti-Labour.

↓ **Source F**
Media mogul Rupert Murdoch heads the list of the most important and influential figures in the media in the UK.

Advertising

Advertising in the media is big business. In the advertising world, television has long been regarded as the most powerful means of persuasion. A single commercial in *Coronation Street* reaches huge audiences. Competition from dozens of other television channels and the Internet means television's mass audience is reducing, so advertisers are turning to other media to help reach potential customers.

Surprisingly, a much older advertising medium – the billboard – is claiming it has the greatest impact. Posters such as 'Hello Boys' for *Wonderbra*, and the controversial *Benetton* adverts (see Source G) show that this medium can be even more powerful than television.

Television is also under threat from the Internet which is attracting viewers away from television – and many website owners want to attract advertisers too.

The purpose of any advertisement is to influence choice or opinion. Some of the techniques used are:

- creating a need and raising expectations
- presenting a particular image
- using peer pressure
- associating a product with role models or celebrities.

Discussions are underway to draw up a single set of advertising rules for the whole of Europe, prompted by the growth of satellite television and Internet advertising. In light of the attempts to ban tobacco promotion, some sections of the advertising industry also wonder how much longer it will be before adverts for potentially risky products, such as alcohol or fast cars, are banned.

Pressure groups, charities and even governments use hard-hitting images and slogans. An advert for the children's charity Barnardos, showing a baby preparing to inject itself with heroin, was blocked by the Committee of Advertising Practice. The Royal Society for the Prevention of Cruelty to Animals (RSPCA) once topped the Advertising Standards Authority's (ASA) poll of 'offensive' adverts, after it used a dead pony to illustrate the European trade in horsemeat.

TASKS

According to the ASA's Code of Practice, an advert must be legal, decent, honest and truthful.

1. Take any magazine or newspaper and highlight all the adverts.
   a) Estimate how much space is given up to advertising.
   b) In pairs or small groups, choose five adverts. Discuss the adverts, and decide whether you think:
      i) they are successful in persuading people to buy the products
      ii) the advertisers have stayed in line with the ASA's code.
2. Pick a product that is advertised in at least two of the following media: television, Internet, radio, newspapers or magazines. Compare how the product is advertised in each medium.

The Italian clothing firm *Benetton* is used to having its advertising campaigns accused of bad taste. Its 'shockvertising' methods, tackling topics such as war, Aids, racism, religion and execution seem to work. No matter how 'tasteless', product demand generally goes up after one of its campaigns.

↑ **Source G**
Benetton 'Shockvertising' advert.

Censorship

Most people believe that it is important that the media is objective and allowed to exercise 'freedom of expression'. A key question is, should this 'freedom' be restrained or censored? Is it right to allow the media to show anything? Does freedom of expression allow intrusion into people's private lives or revealing state secrets?

The problem is where to draw the line. How much should the public be entitled to know or see?

US

We have … reporting guidelines/press briefings

We … take out/eliminate/dig in

We launch … first strikes

Our troops are … professional/cautious/loyal/brave

We … precision bomb

Our missiles cause … collateral damage

Our leaders are … resolute/statesmanlike/assured

THEM

They have … censorship/propaganda

They … destroy/kill/cower in their foxholes

They launch … sneaky missile attacks

Their troops are … brainwashed/cowardly/blindly obedient/fanatical

They … fire wildly at anything

Their missiles cause … civilian casualties

Their leaders are … defiant/evil/monsters

↑ **Source H**
The language of war.

Propaganda and bias

"When war is declared, truth is the first casualty."
Arthur Ponsonby, British diplomat and writer.

What is the media's duty in war? Should it be objective and independent, or be patriotic and support its country? Probably every conflict is fought on at least two grounds: on the battlefield and in the minds of the people influenced by propaganda. Public support for a war can easily disappear if the media is not 'on side'.

The 'good guys' and the 'bad guys' can often both be guilty of misleading their people by being 'economical with the truth' and by using propaganda. In war coverage the media plays a crucial role. It is not simply 'hard facts' that are transmitted through the world's media

systems, but also claims and counter claims, guesses and speculation, censorship and disinformation. Reporting on a war puts the journalist to the test. Pressure to be first with the news has to be met within the context of sensitivity, accuracy and strict guidelines on reporting.

Since the 1991 Gulf conflict, which was described as a 'media-saturated' war, most conflicts throughout the world are televised media events. The results of bombing raids are often filmed and then replayed at press briefings. In the war against terrorism fought in Afghanistan in 2001, John Simpson (a BBC reporter) and his camera crew entered the city of Kabul ahead of the allied troops! People are increasingly concerned that wars can almost become a spectator sport for the viewer.

The military often restricts what information is given to the media and therefore what the public are told. Now a new language is being used by the media to soften the reality of war. During recent conflicts the language used to describe the actions of the British armed forces is totally different from the language used to describe enemy action (see Source H).

Legislation

In Britain, the government has introduced several laws that make all forms of the media accountable for the information it gives out. For example:

- The Obscene Publications Act 1959 and 1964 gives police and other authorities the power to search, confiscate and destroy 'obscene' publications and to prosecute those possessing them.
- The Official Secrets Act 1989 concentrates on the protection of official information. Any journalist or member of the public disclosing this sort of information can be prosecuted.
- The Broadcasting Act 1990 makes provisions to ensure programmes are of a high quality and are suitable for viewing.

The global use of the Internet, however, presents many difficulties for legislation and accountability of the media. Internet use has transformed the media debate. There are many problems in censoring and monitoring information from the Internet. Certain online monitoring, screening, and other controlling technologies are suggested but all of them face strong objections, in terms of practicality and intrusion of privacy.

Accountability

The media is powerful and influential but it is accountable to certain bodies. There are a number of watchdog bodies that regulate and control the various activities of the media. Bodies such as the Broadcasting Complaints Commission, Press Complaints Commission, the British Board of Film Classification and the Advertising Standards Authority perform the following roles:

- monitor standards
- handle complaints from the public
- make recommendations following enquiries
- ensure that the media operates within the law.

In 2001 it was announced in the Queen's Speech that a single regulator for the media and communications industries would be created by 2003. The establishment of the Office of Communications (Ofcom) would reduce the number of regulators in the sector from five to one, taking over the roles of the Independent Television Commission, the Office of Telecommunications (Oftel), the Broadcasting Standards Commission, the Radio Authority and the Radio-communications Agency.

At times the power of the public appears to be limited but in the end, as consumers, individuals can do something. They can always exert pressure by not buying a particular publication or by pressing the 'off' button on their television, radio or computer.

GCSE CHECK

Importance of the media's role in society, including the Internet, in providing information, presenting ideas and affecting opinion

Ability to compare information from different sources

Knowledge of the media's role in shaping our perceptions of the world

TASK

Having read this section and undertaken some of the activities, how influential and powerful do you think that the media is?

Freedom of the media –
why should there be any
limits **?**

Aim

You will:

- appreciate how topical issues are portrayed in the media
- explore the difference between 'need to know' and 'right to know'
- analyse the case for and against media censorship.

> "Everyone has the right to freedom of opinion and expression; this right includes freedom to hold opinions without interference and to seek, receive and impart information and ideas through any media and regardless of frontiers."
>
> **Article 19 of the United Nations Universal Declaration of Human Rights**

It is often claimed that it is the duty of the media to keep people informed about what is going on in the world and in their own country. Despite this, censorship is commonplace in many countries throughout the world: plays, films and books have to be submitted to a government censor before they are released to the general public. In a similar way press releases and radio and television broadcasts are carefully monitored to make sure the 'correct' viewpoints are being given.

You might be surprised to learn that, although the details might change, the story in most countries throughout the world remains the same. The smallest things upset the censors. In certain parts of the world items which to many of us appear to be harmless are censored.

In the UK the authorities do not go as far as some of the examples in Source A, but there is still censorship of the media.

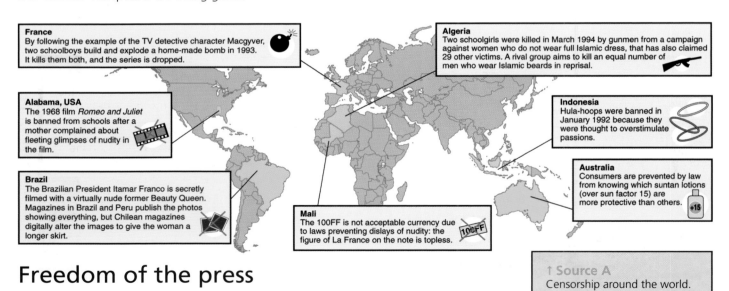

France
By following the example of the TV detective character Macgyver, two schoolboys build and explode a home-made bomb in 1993. It kills them both, and the series is dropped.

Alabama, USA
The 1968 film *Romeo and Juliet* is banned from schools after a mother complained about fleeting glimpses of nudity in the film.

Brazil
The Brazilian President Itamar Franco is secretly filmed with a virtually nude former Beauty Queen. Magazines in Brazil and Peru publish the photos showing everything, but Chilean magazines digitally alter the images to give the woman a longer skirt.

Algeria
Two schoolgirls were killed in March 1994 by gunmen from a campaign against women who do not wear full Islamic dress, that has also claimed 29 other victims. A rival group aims to kill an equal number of men who wear Islamic beards in reprisal.

Indonesia
Hula-hoops were banned in January 1992 because they were thought to overstimulate passions.

Australia
Consumers are prevented by law from knowing which suntan lotions (over sun factor 15) are more protective than others.

Mali
The 100FF is not acceptable currency due to laws preventing dislays of nudity: the figure of La France on the note is topless.

↑ Source A
Censorship around the world.

Freedom of the press

Should there be limits on press freedom? In some countries the public is kept in the dark as the media faces heavy censorship. Other countries adopt a more relaxed attitude, believing either that the public is told what it needs to know or that the public has a right to know everything. Opinions vary about what the press should be allowed to print.

In 2001 the *Mirror* was criticised as irresponsible when it published the headline 'Panic' in reaction to the terrorist threat of anthrax poisoning. In 1997 the *Daily Mail* was applauded for naming five individuals, who were not convicted in court, of being suspected murderers.

Source B
Responsible or irresponsible reporting? Front page of *The Mirror* (October 2001) and the headline from *The Daily Mail* (February 1997).

Generally in the UK the press has freedom in reporting but there are still various forms of press censorship:

- Under the Obscene Publications Act, a newspaper or publisher can be charged with a criminal offence if something is published that is considered as obscene.
- The government can issue a 'D-notice' under the Official Secrets Act to prevent the press from publishing anything classed as an official secret. During war the press is asked not to reveal information about troop movements.
- Defamation of character (libel when written, slander when spoken). If the press publishes an article about someone that is untrue, that person can sue them for damages.
- Contempt of Court. In 2001 newspaper editors were informed that they would be held in contempt of court and face a prison sentence if details were published about the new identities or the whereabouts of the two killers of James Bulger when they were released.

TASKS

1. If you were a newspaper editor, which of the following headlines would you not allow to be published? You will need to look carefully at the four areas of press censorship outlined above before making your decisions. Explain the reasons behind your decisions.
   - 'Famous author is a lying moron'
   - 'British troops planning to attack military base'
   - 'Bulger killers – new identities revealed'
2. Read the following views and decide which one you agree with most. Give reasons for your choice.

I've no doubt the public is interested in the private lives of celebrities; but we've no right to know how they conduct themselves in private. They have the same right as anyone else to protection from intrusion and the telephoto lenses of the paparazzi.

People in the public eye do very nicely out of all the publicity they receive. If they are up to something naughty they only have themselves to blame if the press finds out and splashes them all over the front pages. They can't invite publicity one minute and then the next minute object about their privacy being invaded. They can't have it both ways.

'Chequebook journalism'

Sometimes payments are made to persuade people to supply 'exclusive' information or sell the exclusive rights to their story. 'Chequebook journalism', involving 'exclusives' or 'kiss and tell' stories usually boosts the circulation and profits of a newspaper.

It is not a criminal offence to sell or buy a story; however, the legal process can be put in jeopardy if witnesses or suspects in criminal cases receive payments for telling their story. Lawyers can easily challenge the evidence given by someone if they can show he or she was paid by a journalist. If there is evidence to suggest that the result of a trial may be prejudiced by the actions of a newspaper, a judge may halt the proceedings and action can be taken under the Contempt of Court Act 1981. This says that an offence is committed if a publication 'creates a substantial risk that the course of justice in particular proceedings will be seriously impeded or prejudiced'.

It is estimated that up to 19 witnesses from the 1996 trial of Frederick and Rosemary West received payments for their accounts of the serial killings by the married couple. In one trial that featured an *EastEnders* star, eight national newspapers were accused by the judge of 'unlawful, misleading, scandalous and malicious' reporting. In another case, featuring the pop star Gary Glitter, the prosecution's chief witness struck a deal with the *News of the World* newspaper. She went to the paper with allegations that, when she was 14, the singer had sexually assaulted her. She received £10 000 for her story and the paper also agreed to give her a 'win bonus' of £25 000 if Glitter was found guilty in court on charges of indecent assault. Glitter was not found guilty on that charge.

Source C
The Gary Glitter trial raised important issues for the media. The press was warned over witness payments.

One defence of these 'cash for court confessions' is that without them, some witnesses would not come forward. Critics argue that witnesses may deliberately change their evidence to match with details they gave to the newspaper. Challenges to their reliability could lead to a miscarriage of justice, with a guilty person going free or an innocent person being convicted.

Problems have also arisen in other areas such as purchasing exclusive serialisation rights to a book written by authors with a criminal record. Even paying victims of crime or disasters, or their relatives, to obtain an 'exclusive' may be considered distasteful. Following the Hillsborough tragedy in 1989, relatives of some of the 95 football fans who died were disgusted when they were offered money to tell their stories.

The right of the public to know

In recent years, judges have issued 'gagging orders' preventing the press from publishing certain stories. These 'orders' are often regarded as an attack on press freedom. They also raise a key question: is the story in the public interest or just of interest to the public? There is a difference. Which stories are 'in the public interest' and which are merely 'of interest to the public'?

Since the death of Diana, Princess of Wales, there have been calls for stronger privacy laws preventing the press from publishing stories that invade an individual's privacy. Questions are often asked about media intrusion, and not only into the private lives of public figures. What about the privacy of ordinary individuals who, for whatever reason, find themselves thrown into a media spotlight? Should a line be drawn between the individual's private and public life? When does 'personal become public'? At the moment there is very little legislation to protect an individual's privacy.

TASKS

Good morning, Mrs No-One, I'm a member of the press,
And I'm sorry to disturb you in your hour of distress;
But the public has a right to know just what you've done and seen,
And to help refresh your memory, here's a picture of the Queen ...

With a foot inside your door,
And a chequebook in my hand
For your memoirs I'll agree to pay you up to fifty grand!

Chequebook Journalism by Dillie Keane

1. In your opinion, when does investigation become intrusion?
2. What is meant by a story being 'in the public interest'? Is there any difference between newspapers revealing details of the personal lives of ordinary individuals and those of politicians who claim to have certain family or moral values but do not live up to them?
3. Select a newspaper article about either:
   a) a violent incident, or
   b) a 'celebrity story'.
Edit the article, as though you are a censor, removing any material that you think is not in the 'public interest'. Write a brief report explaining why you removed certain parts – how different is the revised article from the original?

Official secrets

In the last 25 years, there have been several high-profile cases where the UK government has tried to enforce the Official Secrets Act. Sometimes it has been successful but more often it has failed.

In 1985 Clive Ponting, who had worked at the Ministry of Defence, was cleared of breaking the Official Secrets Act. Ponting was charged with leaking a secret document concerning the *General Belgrano*, an Argentinian warship. British forces sank the *Belgrano* during the 1982 Falklands War with the loss of 360 lives. The government insisted that the warship was a direct threat to British forces when it was sunk. The publication of the leaked document showed that the *Belgrano* was less of a threat than the government had claimed.

MI5 and MI6 are the popular names for the Security Service in Britain. MI5 (the Security Service) covers internal security and counterintelligence in the UK. MI6 (the Secret Intelligence Service) covers all areas outside the UK.

Critics believe that the intelligence services are the real power that decides what goes on in this country – they are free to do whatever they want and very few people are allowed to know what they get up to. Supporters insist that secrecy is very important and that the actions that MI5 and MI6 undertake are to protect citizens from threats such as terrorism and espionage.

There was controversy in 1987 when a former MI5 officer, Peter Wright, published his memoirs – *Spycatcher*. The government stated that Wright was forbidden from writing about his MI5 work because it was 'top secret'. Two newspapers were stopped from serialising the book but it was published in America and Australia. Despite the government's efforts, copies came into the UK (see Source D). Attempts to have Wright arrested and brought back from Australia failed. A House of Lords judgement in 1988 overturned the decision to stop the media from reporting anything from former intelligence officers.

Source D
Peter Wright –
Spycatcher.

By 2001 few protests were heard when Stella Rimington, the former head of MI5, produced her memoirs.

In 1997 a former MI6 officer, Richard Tomlinson, was sentenced to a year in prison for passing secrets to an Australian publisher. Another former agent, David Shayler, was charged with breaking the Official Secrets Act after an article about his time in the intelligence services was published in the *Mail on Sunday*.

In 1999 Tomlinson was again in the news when he named agents of the Secret Intelligence Service (SIS), formerly known as MI6, on his Swiss website. Tomlinson also included information on secret service training and methods. When the UK government obtained a legal order against him he just moved to America and again threatened to publish sensitive information.

Technological advances and an increase in 'chequebook journalism' mean the Official Secrets Act is no longer a good safeguard against ex-spies who want to tell their stories. In the Internet age, it appears that the UK authorities cannot do much to stop them as websites can be set up and read anywhere in the world.

Television censorship

Obviously, television is covered by similar censorship regulations as the press, but there are some additional regulations. The 'watershed' refers to a voluntary code of practice under which the television companies agree not to screen programmes considered unsuitable for children until after 9:00pm. This self-censorship even extends to adverts that might cause children distress.

The 1990 Broadcasting Act requires the Independent Television Committee (ITC) to keep a close watch to ensure that programmes do not 'offend against good taste or decency'. For example, the ITC's own code of conduct requires that there should be no abusive treatment of religious views or beliefs and no 'improper exploitation of any susceptibilities of those watching programmes'. In addition, the Advertising Standards Authority checks that all television adverts are 'legal, decent, honest and truthful', and any companies sponsoring programmes must be suitable for the subject content of the programme.

The BBC is controlled by its charter, which requires it to produce programmes that uphold the standards of public decency. The BBC has its own Programme Complaints Unit. This investigates any complaint by members of the public about programmes that might have given an unbalanced view, been biased or offended standards of decency.

Advertising censorship

The Advertising Standards Authority keeps a close watch on all UK media advertising. In 2001 it received 730 complaints about a controversial billboard advert showing a naked female model. The poster was banned for breaking the British Codes of Advertising and Sales Promotion. It was described as sexually suggestive, 'degrading' to women and likely to cause 'serious or widespread offence' (see Source E). In 2000 the European Court of Justice blocked the UK government's attempt to ban tobacco advertising.

Source E ↑

In 2001 posters featuring a naked model were withdrawn. In 2000 the UK government moved to ban tobacco promotion. These two examples increase the debate over which products can – and cannot – be legally advertised. And should governments – or the European Union – have the power to decide?

TASKS

1. 'Censorship is a price worth paying to protect our country's secrets.' Discuss whether the media should be restricted in what they disclose.
2. Make a survey of violence on television. Choose one channel and watch it for the same hour each day for a week, for example between 8:00pm to 9:00pm.
   a) Calculate the number of minutes of violence you see each day.
   b) Make a table with your figures, listing the different types of violence – for example, domestic violence, muggings, fights between individuals, war films or violent behaviour on the professional football pitch.
   c) Calculate the proportion of violent acts where the offender seems to escape punishment or criticism.
   d) Compare your findings with a partner who has studied a different channel.

Film censorship

Sex, violence and swearing seem to be as much a part of today's cinema experience as queues, popcorn and multiplexes. In the UK, films must be submitted to the British Board of Film Classification (BBFC) for a viewing category. By law, these categories must be enforced by cinema owners. The Board's censors can recommend cutting film scenes considered too sexually graphic or violent. It can refuse to grant a certificate and, in addition, local councils can refuse permission for such films to be shown in their area. The BBFC also classifies videos, DVDs and video games. The board takes a hard line on DVDs and videos because children can see them more easily and scenes can be played over and over.

The majority of the cuts made by the BBFC fall into one of the following areas:

- Sexual violence – there is a strict policy on material that seeks to exploit sexual violence.
- Emphasis on violence or sadism – most notably in scenes of torture where violence is presented as prolonged enjoyment.
- Sexual explicitness that falls foul of the obscenity law. This was at issue with the 2001 release of the French film *Romance*, which was described as 'philosophical rather than pornographic'.

→Source F
Film violence put in the dock! A film poster for *Natural Born Killers*.

The case for media censorship

Media censorship is usually justified by some or all of the following arguments:

- Some evidence shows that children and vulnerable individuals can be influenced by what they see.
  - People have a right not to be confronted with sex scenes, violence or obscene language on their televisions.
    - Film and television directors, newspaper publishers and advertisers should not make money from satisfying someone's crude needs.
      - The media should be stopped from intruding on people's privacy. Famous people should have a right to a private life.

The case against media censorship

Those who argue against censorship often hold the following views:

- Democracy needs freedom of information. How can people make informed decisions if facts are kept from them?
- Who decides what needs to be kept secret or what needs to be censored? Who checks that their decision is correct?
- If obscenity and violence are so corrupting, the censors should be very corrupt. After all, they spend their lives watching such things!
- Internet technology has helped make effective censorship impossible.
- Privacy laws can be, and have been used by powerful people (for example, the disgraced media mogul Robert Maxwell) to cover up their misdeeds.

When making its decisions, the BBFC keeps in mind certain laws such as:

- the Obscene Publications Act, concerning material which is likely to be depraving or corrupting
- blasphemy
- criminal libel
- the treatment of animals
- representation of children.

Occasionally, certain films that are released are controversial, and it is not always easy to understand the reasoning behind what is permitted and what is not. It is argued that violent films can affect 'vulnerable' individuals, and there will always be some people who are easily influenced by these films. The films *Natural Born Killers* (see Source F), *Child's Play* and *Reservoir Dogs* have been singled out as contributing to real-life incidents of 'copycat' murders.

Despite the fuss over controversial releases in recent years, the BBFC rarely refuses certificates.

The theatre is also censored by the same obscenity and defamation laws as television and the press. Many theatres, however, have a policy of making sure the public is aware that a performance may cause offence, or is unsuitable for children.

TASK

Based on your understanding of the issues covered in this study, how far do you think the media needs to be censored?

GCSE CHECK

Recognise the importance of a free press	Consider own stance in relation to topical examples of other people's decisions	Bias is fully, clearly and critically evaluated, with reference to specific examples

How can you live in an
information society ?

Aim

You will:

- appreciate the difficulties in keeping your privacy in an information age
- explore some of the arguments given for the need for surveillance
- analyse how technology can threaten your fundamental right to privacy.

'Information is power, and power is control.'

Privacy outside the home is almost extinct. Living in the UK today means you have almost no secrets. Whether using the Internet, the bank cashpoint, walking down the street or even driving on roads, almost your every move is observed or recorded. The question is often asked: Is there anything that can be done about our loss of privacy?

The vast majority of people voluntarily give out their phone numbers and addresses when they allow themselves to be listed in a phone book or fill in details on a form. Some of us go a lot further than that. We register our whereabouts every time we use a bank cashpoint machine. We are regularly monitored by speed cameras on the roads. Ordering goods by mail order makes our shopping habits public knowledge. Whenever we visit websites we are monitored by computers.

The UK is the largest user of Closed Circuit Television (CCTV) in the world. Even the most basic cameras are capable of reading a newspaper headline from 100m away. Since the first CCTV system was installed in 1949 the network is now so dense that in many urban areas people may be monitored from the moment they step out of their front door (see Source B). Some CCTV systems have been linked up to software that can intelligently scan and recognise faces. The images taken by this 'Face Recognition' system can then be checked against a database of known criminals.

↓ Source A
'Every step you take, every move you make, I'll be watching you.'

Source B

"Often the ration of cameras is so high that nobody can escape being filmed unless they avoid shopping, refuse to dine out and never visit the cinema, theatre or go clubbing. On an average day in any big city, an individual is filmed by more than 300 cameras from 30 different CCTV networks."

Adapted from an article, 'Smile, you're on 300 candid cameras' in *The Sunday Times* by Dipesh Gadher (1999)

Source C

Big Brother is always watching us

Bank cashpoints

Every time an individual uses an Automated Teller Machine (ATM) the time, date, details and location of the transaction are recorded by the bank.

Electoral register

Details like an individual's birth date and address are available to any member of the public. In the past, local councils have been obliged by law to sell their electoral register to anyone who asks. In November 2001 a High Court judge ruled that selling the register without giving individual electors a right of objection was a 'breach of privacy' – but electors still need to formally opt out.

Using a phone

The phone company automatically records the number being called and how long the conversation lasts.

Credit cards

Everything charged to your card is recorded on a database that the police, among others, could look at.

Supermarket scanners

When a store card is used everything you purchase is recorded. In this way your shopping habits can be easily assessed.

Email

Employers can read any emails sent from the workplace. In 1999 five workers at *Rolls Royce* in Bristol were fired and ten more punished after nude pictures were emailed from its workstations. However, the firm ignored the fact that pornographic magazines were freely on sale in its site shop!

Cookies

Many websites tag visitors with 'magic cookies' that record what you are looking at and when you have been surfing.

CCTV

There are over one million cameras in the UK.

What do we get in return? We get security walking down the streets, less vandalism, safer driving as some motorists are wary of being caught speeding and the convenience of cash when we need it.

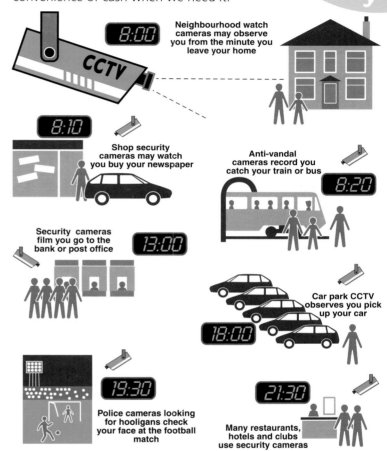

↑ Source D

Privacy – the price you pay! Listening in to your phone calls, watching your shopping habits, taking your photo and reading your emails.

TASKS

1. According to Source B, how can you avoid being caught on CCTV?
2. How do you think the authorities decide where to place CCTV? What factors do they have to consider when making their choices?
3. Choose three of the eight ways in which we can be watched (see Source C) and try to explain both the advantages and disadvantages of having this monitoring.

How can you protect yourself?

All you have to do is follow certain precautions. These will certainly help protect your privacy a little bit.

- Whenever possible, pay cash rather than use credit or debit cards.
- Remember that when buying through mail order, some companies may sell their customer lists.
- Remember that when filling out warranty cards on items you buy, this is a 'data mine' for market researchers.
- Use only payphones or a pre-pay mobile phone that does not require you to give an address when you buy it.
- Consider changing to an Internet service provider that you can use anonymously, and which does not give you a fixed net address.
- Protect your email messages with encryption software.
- Look on application forms for a 'tick box' to stop your details being passed on.

- Avoid driving and going out shopping, clubbing or eating in busy cities!
- The final way of protecting yourself is to make use of the law:
  - The Data Protection Act – if anybody misuses your personal information, if they sell it on without your permission, if they keep it far longer than necessary or refuse you access, you can have them prosecuted.
  - The Trade Descriptions Act – if someone promises you that they are going to give you privacy and they do not fulfil their promise, they are liable under criminal law for prosecution.

No-one suggested keeping your privacy in an information age is easy! Just when you thought you might be coping with all this, along comes a further development which you really cannot do much against. Especially since it has the protection of the law.

Electronic surveillance

In the last few years, laws have been introduced to cope with the increasing use of electronic forms of communication. The fear is that laws designed to catch computer criminals could result in a huge increase in the amount of secret surveillance carried out on everyone.

The controversial Regulation of Investigatory Powers Act 2000 can also require Internet companies to install equipment which enables every piece of a subscriber's communication traffic – website visits, purchases, downloads, as well as emails sent and received – to be linked to a government monitoring centre. This allows up to one in 10 000 of their customers to be watched and allows police and intelligence services to quickly turn on wiretaps or intercept Internet-transmitted data from suspects. The only organisations exempt are Communication Service Providers (CSPs) servicing financial companies.

The Act was criticised almost from the moment it was introduced. Security experts, privacy watchdogs and pressure groups fear that this power could lead to a large increase in wiretaps, threatening the fundamental rights to privacy of many individuals. The fear is that the intelligence services will be able to look for any 'suspicious' activities rather than restrict surveillance to certain individuals suspected of criminal activities.

Government officials insist that although the technology exists to secretly monitor thousands of people using phones, fax machines and the Internet, this does not mean that all these potential wiretaps will actually be used. Critics point out that any interference with communications is an abuse of a fundamental human right, as guaranteed by the European Convention on Human Rights.

Not surprisingly, many people are concerned that their privacy is at risk as our lives become ever more dependent on computers and online information.

How can you live in an information society?

Government plans to put all its services online by 2005 have highlighted how our lives are becoming ever more dependent on computers and online information.

The Information Commissioner's Report (2001) revealed that 96% of individuals rated their personal privacy rights as important or very important. The report mentioned 15 case studies involving unlawful use of data. Examples included:

■ a telecoms employee who passed information to a friend about a female customer's telephone account

■ data gained by deception from the vehicle licensing agency

■ an employee who unlawfully copied a customer database to use when he established his own company.

The Report highlighted several areas where our privacy is at risk, warning that safeguards are essential for data protection.

Source E

"Cybercrime – developments in communications, particularly the Internet and mobile phones, have provided new opportunities for criminals. Not surprisingly law enforcement agencies want the ability to access these communications for surveillance. ... This access must be limited to cases where the need justifies the privacy intrusion.

One area where the consequences of poor data quality can be particularly serious is the Police National Computer. ... The situation is becoming critical due to the establishment of the Criminal Records Bureau, which will issue criminal record certificates to employers. There is a real risk that details of actual convictions may not appear on certificates and that successful appeals may not be taken into account.

Monitoring of employees, in particular the monitoring of their emails and Internet access, has drawn much comment. Any monitoring must address the specific risks that an employer faces, it must be a proportionate response to those risks, conducted with no more intrusion than necessary and employers must be open with their employees about its existence."

**Extracts from the Information Commissioner's
Annual Report (2001)**

TASKS

1. What are the main concerns of the Report regarding the use of the Police National Computer?
2. What recommendations does the Report make regarding the monitoring of employees?
3. How useful are the suggestions (see page 140) given about how you can protect yourself? Are they practical?

Echelon

Imagine a global spying network that can eavesdrop on every single phone call, fax or email, anywhere on the planet. It might appear to be like a scene from a James Bond film, but despite denials, it does exist. The power of the American National Security Agency (nicknamed 'No Such Agency'!) is amazing.

One of the largest National Security Agency (NSA) systems is called Echelon – a vast international electronic eavesdropping network using super computers run by the intelligence organisations of America, the UK, Canada, Australia and New Zealand. The network is so secret that the British and American governments have only recently admitted that it even existed.

In May 2001, a European Parliament committee advised all computer users to encrypt their emails if they wanted to avoid being spied on by Echelon. Many experts believe that the use of Echelon, which is capable of over two million intercepts per hour, is against the European Human Rights Convention, which guarantees privacy to all individuals.

On the North Yorkshire moors around 30 giant radomes rise from the American military base at Menwith Hill. Inside each is the world's most sophisticated eavesdropping technology, capable of listening in to satellites. The base is linked directly to the headquarters of the American NSA at Fort Meade in Maryland, and it is also linked to a series of other listening posts scattered across the world, like Britain's own spy centre, GCHQ in Cheltenham.

The first Echelon network was built in 1971, but it has regularly been updated since then. It can be used to intercept almost any electronic communication – any phone conversation, Internet browsing history, or satellite transmission. Every day it sifts through all the data it can collect from over 90% of all Internet traffic, reading millions of emails and faxes sent by ordinary people.

The network homes in on a long list of key words, phrases, addresses, names or patterns of messages – anything the intelligence services think could be 'suspicious', or linked to international crime like terrorism.

Living in an information society is not easy. Worrying developments are seen such as the Regulation of Investigatory Powers Act and the power of intelligence agencies. Individuals and companies who are concerned that they are being spied on use encryption. This means that if they want their emails and faxes to remain private they encode them. Sending an unencrypted email is basically like posting a letter without an envelope.

Critics believe that the new powers of intelligence agencies undermine the usefulness of encryption codes. It also raises severe problems for areas such as e-commerce which can only be successful if everyone involved is confident in the security of the transaction. Some companies would consider moving abroad to operate in countries which refuse to allow such powers.

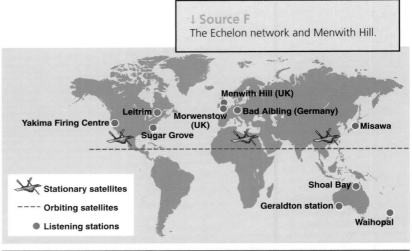

↓ Source F
The Echelon network and Menwith Hill.

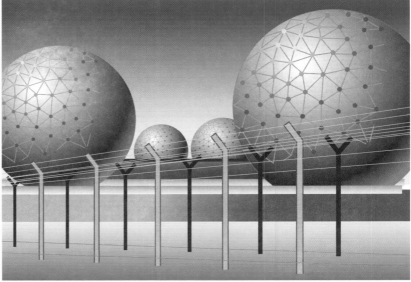

TASKS

Look at Source F and read through Source G.

1. In Case Study 1 you learnt about the ways in which emotive language can be used to get a reaction from the reader. Try to pick out any words or phrases in Source G which you believe could be described as emotive language.

2. Are the concerns expressed about Echelon outweighed by the advantages that our society gains by its existence?

3. If you controlled Echelon, what words and phrases would you watch out for? Make a list. Now think how many times you have used these words or phrases in a phone conversation or in an email. How do you feel about the thought that someone might have been listening in on your communications?

Source G

A story about the future!

"This is a story about the future. It's a story about the gleaming new world of technology, of infinite data, of a brave new information society brimming with machines that process and deliver the world quickly, cheaply and efficiently. A world crammed with technology that intimately knows each one of us. But this won't be a pleasant story – it is a nightmare! The future will deliver the death of privacy. And with the death of privacy will come a new era of control over our lives, our movements and our lifestyles."

From *Counterblast: The Death of Privacy*
presented by Simon Davies

Email

Email is so quick and easy but just one badly-aimed mouse click can send an email message to the wrong person. As for confidentiality, many companies automatically scan the contents of employees' emails; some computer viruses send copies of emails you have previously sent to other addresses stored on your computer; and then eavesdropping systems like Echelon can scan the content of every email sent anywhere in the world. If you want an email or fax to remain private you should encode them – to decode the information the receiver must have the 'encyption keys' needed to decode the information.

TASKS

1. Work in small groups to conduct a research project on the topic 'Is the new information age a nightmare scenario?'
You will need to:
a) Research 'privacy and information laws' and surveillance technology using the Internet, library or any other research sources.
b) Conduct questionnaires which examine people's attitudes to living in an 'information society'. How aware are people of the number of ways they are monitored?

c) Present findings in appropriate IT forms, such as a PowerPoint presentation or web page on your school Intranet.

2. You cannot have a situation where terrorist groups and serious criminal gangs can have a means of communication which is untouchable and completely secure. To compete with the criminals, the law enforcement agencies must have the 'tools to do the job'. Do you agree? Give reasons for your answer.

GCSE CHECK

Recognise the right of the media to investigate, and to report upon, issues of public interest subject to the law	Read and synthesise information from different sources	Form and express an opinion in writing and analyse and present evidence

Glossary

Act of Parliament
A bill which has passed all 5 stages (first reading, second reading, committee stage, report stage, third reading) in both the House of Commons and House of Lords, and received Royal Assent.

Anthrax
An infectious disease that causes fever and either pneumonia or severe skin ulcers, and may be fatal.

Apathy
A lack of interest or enthusiasm. Apathy comes from the Greek a [without] + pathos [feeling].

ATM
Automatic Teller Machine, more usually known in the UK as a cashpoint.

Autopsy
An examination of a dead body to find out the cause of death.

Blatant
Very obvious or noticeable.

Boycott
To refuse to have any dealings or contact with a company, country or individual as a form of disapproval.

British Youth Council
The representative body for young people in the UK. An independent charity, it is run for and by young people and works to represent their views to central and local government, political parties, pressure groups and the media.

The Childrens' Rights Alliance for England
An alliance of over 170 organisations committed to promoting childrens' human rights.

National Youth Agency
Aims to advance youth work to promote young peoples' personal and social development, and their voice, influence and place in society. Funded primarily by the Local Government Association and government departments.

Cabinet
Group of ministers in charge of the various departments of government who meet regularly with the Prime Minister.

CCTV
Closed-circuit television. Surveillance or security cameras used within buildings and on public streets.

Church of England
The official state Church of England with Queen Elizabeth II as its head, it originated when Henry VIII broke away from the Roman Catholic Church in the 16th century.

Citizens' Charter
A set of proposals drawn up by the government or local authority outlining minimum acceptable standards of service, and peoples' rights connected with public bodies.

CND
The Campaign for Nuclear Disarmament, an organisation formed in 1958 to oppose Britain's development of nuclear weapons.

Colonialism
A policy of acquiring colonies, often simply as a source of income and profit.

Commission for Racial Equality
A publicly funded, non-governmental body set up under the Race Relations Act 1976 to tackle racial discrimination and promote racial equality. It works in both the public and private sectors to encourage fair treatment and to promote equal opportunities for everyone.

Commonwealth of Nations
Formerly called the British Commonwealth, a voluntary organisation of 53 states which were once imperial possessions of Britain with the reigning British monarch as head.

Community
A group of people brought together by a common religion, nationality or occupation.

Constituency
A district represented by a Member of Parliament.

Constitution
A set of rules governing an organisation, or the laws and rights of a country's people. Written constitutions normally describe government institutions and their powers, ways to amend the constitution, and a bill of rights.

Contempt of Court
Disregard of or disrespect for the rules of a court of law.

Crown Prosecution Service
The Crown Prosecution Service is responsible for prosecuting people in England and Wales charged by the police with a criminal offence.

Curfew
An order or rule that forbids people to be on the streets after a certain hour.

Custody
Arrest or imprisonment, or the act of placing someone – often a child – under an individual's responsibility for their care and protection.

Defendant
The person against whom a charge is brought in court.

Democracy
A form of government where the people govern themselves or elect representatives to govern them.

Direct democracy
A form of government under which the public vote directly on many of the issues, unlike a representative democracy where the public votes for MPs or councillors to take all the decisions for them.

Direct Rule
Period from March 1972 to December 1999 when Northern Ireland was governed from Westminster. Conservative Prime Minster Edward Heath had decided to strip the parliament of its power and introduce direct rule from Westminster as a response to the worsening security situation in Northern Ireland.

'Dumbing down'
A process of significantly lowering standards.

Eastern Bloc
Group of Communist countries mainly in Eastern Europe.

Electoral Reform Society
An organisation which campaigns for the strengthening of democracy in the UK through changes to the voting system and electoral arrangements.

Faith Schools
Primary and Secondary schools set up, run by and normally exclusively attended by members of one particular religious faith.

'First Past the Post'
An electoral system in which the winner is whoever gets most votes.

Global interdependence
A belief that the actions and decisions of each individual nation inevitably affect the welfare and fortunes of all, and that therefore all nations should work with awareness and consideration of others.

Good Friday Agreement
A breakthrough document in the history of Northern Ireland. Signed in 1998 it sought to address relationships within Northern Ireland, between Northern Ireland and the Republic; and between both parts of Ireland and England, Scotland and Wales. The final Agreement was put to a referendum in Northern Ireland and in the Irish Republic. The result was overwhelmingly in favour of the Agreement: 71.2% of people in Northern Ireland and 94.39% in the Republic voted Yes to accepting the Agreement.

Green Paper
A statement of the government's proposals or policies on a specific issue, usually the basis for discussion and consultation.

Green-belt
Land usually surrounding a town or city where building is very strictly controlled, or even prevented entirely.

Hansard
The official record of speeches made in the House of Commons, published since 1774.

Harassment
To annoy, trouble, pester a person constantly, or frequently.

Heritage
The cultural traditions of a nation.

Home Office
Government department dealing with law and order.

House of Commons
The lower elected assembly containing 650 members each representing a constituency, and elected for a maximum of five years. The House is presided over by the Speaker.

House of Lords
The upper assembly of parliament, for long made up of non-elected members and consisting of hereditary and life peers, and some Church of England bishops. Reform of the House of Lords began in 2000 when the Labour Government announced proposed reforms including removal of hereditary peers and introduction of some elected members.

IMF
International Monetary Fund. Based in Washington, DC and formed in 1945. It has four main aims: to promote international monetary co-operation, expand international trade, stabilise exchange rates and give financial assistance.

Indigenous
Being native to an area, or belonging naturally to a country.

Infrastructure
The basic organization or system of society, or the basic levels of services, equipment etc needed for a country to be able to perform satisfactorily.

Internment
The policy of confinement of selected individuals or types/groups of people, often within a restricted area or prison.

Kyoto Protocol
An agreement signed at Kyoto, Japan in 1997 whereby developed countries committed to reduce their emissions of damaging greenhouse gases. Legally binding only if 55 out of the 160 endorsing countries sign up to it.

Libel
written and published false facts or statements about an individual that damage their reputation

Local Agenda 21
A principle of acting locally while thinking globally that aims to create a society that does not destroy the environment or exploit developing countries. The principle dates back to the Rio Earth Summit in 1992, and in the UK all local authorities are required to have a strategy in place showing how their local actions are influenced by Global Climate Change and Sustainable Development.

MI5
The Security Service in the UK. It's role is to protect national security from terrorism, and espionage, safeguard the economic well-being of the UK against foreign threats, and to support the law enforcement agencies in preventing and detecting serious crime.

MI6
The Secret Intelligence Service in the UK. According to the Intelligence Services Act 1994 the role of MI6 is to provide information about the actions or intentions of persons outside the UK, to perform other tasks relating to the actions or intentions of these persons in relation to the interests of national security, with particular reference to defence and foreign policies.

Naturalization
the process where a country gives national citizenship to an individual who was not born there.

Non-custodial sentences
a judicial sentence that does not involve the imprisonment of the offender.

Orange Order
Developed from the Orange Society (formed in 1795) and named after the Protestant royal line of William of Orange, later William III of Great Britain and Ireland.

Oxfam
UK charity founded in 1942 as the Oxford Committee for Famine Relief, and working towards reducing world poverty.

Partition
Division of a country into two (or more) independent states.

Patriotic
Being loyal or devoted to a country.

Patten Report
An in-depth review of policing in Northern Ireland, carried out in 1998-1999 by the Independent Commission on Policing for Northern Ireland and led by Christopher Patten. The report produced at the end, entitled "A New Beginning: Policing in Northern Ireland" but commonly referred to as The Patten Report, was ground-breaking in terms of its attempt to build a new policing service on a fundamental basis of protecting human rights.

Plaintiff
The person who brings a case against someone else in a court of law.

Prime Minister
The chief minister in a government. The UK Prime Minister works with the Cabinet to reach decisions on policy and is usually the leader of the largest political party in parliament.

Prime Minister's Question Time
Question time in the House of Commons is when issues and grievances are raised by MPs and information sought about the Government's plans. The Prime Minister answers questions at 3.00 pm for half an hour every Wednesday when Parliament is sitting.

Private member's bill
An alternative method of passing legislation in parliament, where Back Bench or Private Members initiate a Bill and may ultimately pass legislation.

Proportional representation
The electoral system where each political party is represented in parliament in proportion to the votes it received in the election.

Ratify
To give formal agreement to, for instance the signing of a treaty.

Referendum
Giving the people the opportunity to state their opinion on a subject or issue through a straight vote for or against it.

Remand
The process of sending someone accused of a crime back into custody until more evidence is collected, and the case can then be tried.

Representative democracies
The democracies where the representatives speak and act on behalf of an electorate.

Returning officer
The official in charge of running an election, counting the votes and announcing the result.

Sectarianism
Loyalty or very excessive attachment or focus to particular party, often used in descriptions of the political situation within Northern Ireland.

Segregation
Enforced separation or systematic isolation of one group, often a racial or ethnic minority.

Sinn Fein
Irish political party developed in the early 20th century to support Irish independence from Britain, and now the main Irish nationalist party.

Slander
False or damaging spoken statement about a person, but legally it may also be any sound or gesture intended to defame.

Statute law
A law made by the legislated assembly of a country and recorded in some form of formal document.

Subjugate
To bring under control, or to make another person or group obedient.

Subsidies
Any sum of money given, for instance by government to agriculture to help with costs or to keep prices low.

Surgery day
A fixed time during which a local MP or councillor makes time to be available to the general public.

Sustainable development
Essentially the idea of ensuring a better quality of life for everyone, now and for generations to come. A widely-used alternative definition is 'development which meets the needs of the present without compromising the ability of future generations to meet their own needs'.

Testimony
A statement made under oath, often in a court of law.

The Refugee Council
The largest organisation in the UK working with asylum seekers and refugees, giving help and support and working with asylum seekers and refugees to ensure their needs and concerns are addressed.

The Troubles
Name given to the period of violent conflict in Northern Ireland beginning with the Civil Rights marches in the late 1960s to the political resolution of the 1998 Good Friday Agreement.

White Paper
A government statement about policy produced for the purpose of informing parliament of government plans & proposals.

World Bank
Also known as the International Bank for Reconstruction and Redevelopment, founded in 1945 to help raise standards of living in developing countries.

Index

Acknowledgements

'Colour Code' by Gary Younge from Red Pepper, June 1997.

All Our Children by Babette Brown, published by BBC Education, 1995.

'The truth about tikka masala' by Iqbal Wahhab from The Independent, 24 April 2001.

'The search for British self-knowledge could end in the usual muddle' by Neil Ascherson from The Independent on Sunday, 2 April 1995.

'Respect for all' by David Blunkett from Connections, Summer 2001.

The Stephen Lawrence Inquiry Report by Sir William MacPherson, published February 1999. © Crown copyright, 1999.

'Pre-riot reports' by Vikram Dodd from The Guardian, 10 July 2001. © The Guardian.

'Votes@16' from The Electoral Reform Society website. Extract reproduced with permission from The Electoral Reform Society.

'Brits come out top in TV watching league' by Clare Cozens from The Guardian, 20 March 2001. © The Guardian.

'Chequebook Journalism' music by Dillie Keane, lyrics by Dillie Keane and Marilyn Cutts. Published with permission of the author, Dillie Keane.

'Smile, you are on 300 candid camaras' by Dipesh Gadher from The Sunday Times, 14 February 1999.

'The Death of Privacy' from Counterblast presented by Simon Davies, produced by the BBC. Quotation published with permission of the presenter.

Community Cohesion: A Report of the Independent Review Team chaired by Ted Cantle. © Crown Copyright, 2001.

'Ocean warriors' by John Vidal from The Guardian, 19 July 2000. © The Guardian.

'Wind power use grows by 30%' by Paul Brown from The Guardian, 10 January 2000. © The Guardian.

'Flood Bush email stalls White House server' by Julia Day from The Guardian, 3 April 2001. © The Guardian.

'British youth most ignorant about the EU' by Ian Black from The Guardian, 8 November 2001. © The Guardian.

'Poll highlights Britons' ignorance over EU' by Patrick Wintour from The Guardian, 6 December 2001. © The Guardian.

'A cure worse than the disease' by Larry Elliott from The Guardian, 21 January 2002. © The Guardian.

'Majority support tests on animals' by Alan Travis and Jill Treanor from The Guardian, 23 January 2001. © The Guardian.

'Animal tests are science not torture' by James Meek from The Guardian, 18 August 2000. © The Guardian.

'Mass slaughter threat to whales' by Anthony Browne from The Observer, 9 April 2000. © The Observer.

'Global Warming Map' from 'Special Reports: Global Warming' from Guardian Unlimited, http://www.guardian.co.uk. © The Guardian.

Address to 'The International Forum on Globalisation's Tech-In' at Seattle, Washington, USA, 27 November 1999.

'Unfinished Business' a Jubilee 2000 Report. Reproduced with permission of Jubilee Plus.

'At the age of 16…' from the Electoral Reform Society website, http://www.electoral-reform.org.uk. Reproduced with permission of the Electoral Reform Society.

Graph: 'ODA as Percentage of GDP, 1998' from the Global Policy Forum website, http://www.globalpolicy.org. Reproduced with permission of the Global Policy Forum.

Chart: 'Measuring Global Poverty: People living on below $1 a day in developing countries, 1987, 1990 and 1998' from Global Economic Prospects and the Developing Countries 2001 by Bill Shaw et al., published by the World Bank, 2001.

Chart: 'Population living on less than $2 per day in developing countries, 1987, 1990 and 1998' from Global Economic Prospects and the Developing Countries 2001 by Bill Shaw et al., published by the World Bank, 2001.

Graph: '2015 Goals and progress made' from Global Economic Prospects and the Developing Countries 2001 by Bill Shaw et al., published by the World Bank, 2001.

'Tough Times for Cocoa Farmers' from the Comic Relief website, http://www.comicrelief.com.

'What's it all about?' from the Comic Relief website, http://www.comicrelief.com

'Shurrup! Who's the MP for round here?' by Sue Townsend from The Observer, 20 May 2001. © Sue Townsend.

Photographs

Cover images: Corbis

Page 5 Digital Stock, Corel, Adam Woolfitt/Corbis, Ric Ergenbright/Corbis; Page 6 Quememer/Corbis, The Sun/Rex Features; Page 7 MSI/Corbis; Page 8 Rex Features, Bettmann/Corbis, Topham/Pressnet; Page 9 PA Photos; Page 12 Steve Eason/Photofusion; Page 16 Topham/PA; Page 19 Topham, PA Photos; Page 20 Popperfoto/Reuters; Page 21 Vehbi Koca/Photofusion, Popperfoto/Reuters; Page 22 Mirrorpix.com; Page 23 Popperfoto/Reuters; Page 25 PA Photos; Page 27 PA Photos; Page 28 Topham/UN; Page 29 Ian Waldie/Reuters; Page 32 PA Photos; Page 33 Brenda Prince/Format; Page 34 Corbis; Page 36 Topham/AP; Page 37 Corbis, John O'Reilly/Rex Features; Page 41 Topham/Photonews; Page 42 Topham/PA; Page 44 PA Photos; Page 45 Ian Hodgson/Reuters; Page 46 Mirrorpix.com; Page 47 Dana Gluckstein/Corbis; Page 54 Topham Picturepoint; Page 55 Electoral Reform Society; Page 56 Corel; Page 59 PA Photos; Page 60 Popperfoto; Page 61 Popperfoto; Page 66 Rex Features; Page 67 Popperfoto/Reuters x2; Page 71 Corbis, Rex Features; Page 73 Corbis; Page 74 AP Photo/Gene Herrick; Page 76 Paula Solloway/Format Photographers; Page 78 PA Photos x2; Page 79 PA Photos; Page 81 Rex Features; Page 84 Rex Features x2; Page 88 Greenpeace; Page 94 Greenpeace; Page 95 Greenpeace; Page 102 ©News International Newspapers Limited, Rex Features; Page 104 Rex Features, Popperfoto/Reuters; Page 109 Mike Hutchings/Reuters; Page 112 Paul Hackett/Reuters 1999; Page 114 Rex Features; Page 117 Rex Features; Page 118 Rex Features, Scott Olson/Reuters; Page 120 Mirrorpix.com; Page 125 Rex Features; Page 126 Corbis; Page 127 The Advertising Archive Ltd.; Page 131 Mirrorpix.com; Page 132 Topham Picturepoint; Page 134 Topham Picturepoint, Peter Brooker/Rex Features; Page 115 The Advertising Archive Ltd.; Page 136 BBFC, Kobal Collection/Warner Bros; Page 138 Gary Carlton/Rex Features